A Study of Petrine Christology from
Key Texts in 2 Peter

A Study of Petrine Christology from
Key Texts in 2 Peter

KELLY ADAIR SEELY

WIPF & STOCK · Eugene, Oregon

A STUDY OF PETRINE CHRISTOLOGY FROM KEY TEXTS IN 2 PETER

Copyright © 2021 Kelly Adair Seely. All rights reserved. Except for brief quotations in critical publications or reviews, no part of this book may be reproduced in any manner without prior written permission from the publisher. Write: Permissions, Wipf and Stock Publishers, 199 W. 8th Ave., Suite 3, Eugene, OR 97401.

Wipf & Stock
An Imprint of Wipf and Stock Publishers
199 W. 8th Ave., Suite 3
Eugene, OR 97401

www.wipfandstock.com

PAPERBACK ISBN: 978-1-7252-9201-7
HARDCOVER ISBN: 978-1-7252-9200-0
EBOOK ISBN: 978-1-7252-9202-4

10/11/21

To Janice, my loving wife, whose sacrificial care allowed me to study long interrupted hours to bring this work to completion. To my parents, Robert and Naida, who always have encouraged me to study the Scriptures carefully; for all the years you supported me physically, spiritually, and financially. To my precious daughters, Helena and Phoebe, who sacrificed many hours of play time with Daddy and inspired me to work hard and finish.

"And I will make every effort so that after my departure you may be able at any time to recall these things."

2 Peter 1:15

Contents

1. Introduction | 1
2. Jesus' Divinity in 2 Peter | 7
3. Jesus' Uniqueness in 2 Peter | 63
4. Conclusion | 109

   Bibliography | 117

1

Introduction

MOTIVATION AND PURPOSE

Christology has not only shaped faith communities over the millennia, but it has also influenced nations and altered their histories. Of great importance is that one's Christology finds shape from the Bible, and not by denominational or religious dogma. Many significant world events (e.g., the crusades, the Münster rebellion) negatively shaped culture and faith due to a faulty Christology. Today, scholars and faith groups alike have conflicting beliefs about Jesus. A need exists to understand a biblical Christology from those who were closest to Jesus. As part of Jesus' inner circle of disciples, the apostle Peter was a major figure in the early church period, as well as in the New Testament. The Gospel writers often highlighted Peter's close relationship to Jesus. One must peer into the actual words of such an apostle to understand more fully the teaching of Christ in the New Testament.

From the period of Athanasius, the teaching about Christ has suffered due to false teaching, whether by act of volition or coercion.[1] Scholars outside the realm of traditional biblical Christianity have attacked some of the orthodox christological positions, such as the deity and uniqueness of Christ. These confrontations span from the period of Hermann Samuel Reimarus[2]

---

1 See Anatolios, "Athanasius' Christology Today."
2 See Klein, *Hermann Samuel Reimarus*.

to Jürgen Becker[3] and Bart Ehrman.[4] Even N. T. Wright, an Anglican scholar, who presented at the 2010 Evangelical Theological Society, has imposed upon traditional biblical Christianity his unorthodox view of Christology, specifically as it pertains to Christ's work and fulfillment of the law.[5]

While the scholarly community has written countless works concerning Christology in the Gospels and Pauline Epistles, few scholars have examined the Christology of the General Epistles. More specifically, the christological debate has neglected 2 Peter. The main reason the Christology of 2 Peter rarely becomes the focus of a sizeable work is the emphasis of the epistle upon eschatology. The wonder of the eschaton and what one can glean from understanding it in 2 Peter frequently overshadowed subtle yet crucial information found in the epistle. Terrance Callan demonstrated this christological understanding in his brief article concerning 2 Peter, in which he wrote:

> Despite the relative neglect of 2 Peter in New Testament scholarship, there have been several recent discussions of its theology. However, none discusses 2 Peter's Christology at any length; all focus on its ethics and eschatology. These are clearly the main concerns of 2 Peter. Nevertheless, 2 Peter's presentation of Christ is also significant.[6]

While the author of this work does not always agree with Callan's theological conclusions, he confidently demonstrated the need for further research concerning the person of Christ in 2 Peter.

Regardless of the neglect of 2 Peter by current scholarship, the christological goldmines of the uniqueness and deity of Christ one finds in 2 Peter demand that space be devoted to the subject. Scholars should not continue to devote the majority of research to a select few works in the New Testament while neglecting precious treasures in others. This work assumes the truth and validity of 2 Timothy 3:16–17 concerning the inspiration and worth of all Scripture. Because the christological teachings of 2 Peter are of great importance to New Testament thought and understanding, one must not abandon them as peripheral or of subsequent importance to other theological themes.

One's Christology directly affects practical application of the gospel. For example, those who hold a faulty Christology in key areas will likely

---

3 See Becker, "Ich bin die Auferstehung."

4 See Ehrman, *Orthodox Corruption of Scripture*.

5 See Wright, *Jesus and the Victory of God*, 660f.; also see Moore, "Who Are the Liberals Now?"; also see Seifrid, "Near Word of Christ."

6 Callan, "Christology of Peter," 253.

err regarding the gospel, which will negatively affect their evangelistic practices. Without an accurate Christology, one is left to call others to follow a man of their own creation rather than Jesus as the Bible describes him. Therefore, a biblical Christology, properly informed by 2 Peter, will have a positive impact on evangelism.

As a core assumption, the author of this book holds that a biblical theology/Christology must inform a systematic theology and not vice versa. The only true way to build a biblical Christology is to expose the text exegetically. It is upon this solidly exegetical and expositional foundation that theologians should base their Christology.

The main goal of this study is to survey the key christological passages in 2 Peter as a means toward an enhancement of a Petrine Christology. Callan identified the two major areas and key passages in his aforementioned article: 1) Jesus' divinity, and 2) Jesus' distinctness from the Father. However, not only was his attempt to deal with the passage only cursory, but his work also had a different goal than establishing a unified Petrine Christology based upon the exegesis of key passages.

This book will contribute further to the field of New Testament theological studies by allowing a solid exegetical/expositional basis for one's theological conclusions. This study will begin with specific exegesis and make christological conclusions.

Second, as a part of this work, the author will pay attention to the implications concerning a unified Petrine Christology. The conservative theological presupposition is that the apostle Peter wrote the letter bearing his name, and the author of this book holds this position.[7] The following work will contribute to this understanding by examining the framework of unity in Peter's Christology. As part of this study, the author will seek to answer whether the Christology of 2 Peter is analogous to that of Peter's christological concerns in other parts of the New Testament.

JUSTIFICATION

Christological research is justified on the basis of no less than five grounds. First, for orthodox Christianity, the christological emphases of Christ's deity and uniqueness, or his distinctiveness from the Father, are ostensible

---

7 As already demonstrated, 2 Peter has its detractors, such as Ehrman, due to issues concerning its authenticity. However, not all scholarship is in agreement that 2 Peter is pseudepigraphic, as Ehrman asserts. Rather, many scholars demonstrate the reliability of 2 Peter's authenticity and authorship. Supporting Petrine authorship are Kruger, "Authenticity of 2 Peter"; Bigg, Critical and Exegetical *Commentary*, 199–247; Green, *Second Epistle General of Peter*, 13–39; Moo, *2 Peter, Jude*, 21–26.

throughout the course of Scripture. The Gospels, the most exhaustive accounts of Jesus' life, are full of references to the deity of Christ. The apostle John clearly holds a high Christology, employing language like θεὸς (God) or ἐκλεκτὸς τοῦ θεοῦ (Son of God) in John 1:1, 34. However, the other three Gospel writers often refer to Jesus' divinity using other terminology or by inference. The importance of terminology and frequent references to Jesus' divinity in the New Testament demands its examination in 2 Peter.

Second, Christ's treatment of his own identity warrants further research into the teaching of who he is. It is important for a scholar and/or pastor to understand specifically who Jesus said he is in order to remain viable in ministry. If Christ is not who he claimed to be, a pastor may find that he practices ministry or studies the Scriptures in vain.

Third, if Peter truly is the author of the second epistle that bears his name, then his perspective concerning the identity of Jesus is very important. If one can determine that Peter wrote the second epistle examining christological language and terminology, then one can have more confidence that the Christology of the epistle comes via one of Christ's closest associates during his earthly ministry.

Fourth, this topic will contribute exegetical information that will inform one's Christology. Regarding the deity and uniqueness of Christ, this research will guard against false assumptions made by theologians employing faulty presuppositions.

Fifth, this justification stems from the great significance of the deity and uniqueness of Christ. Determining a significant piece of biblical Christology is extremely important. A faulty Christology may lead scholars, pastors, and the people they lead and teach to spiritual death.[8] However, a clear understanding of the teaching about Christ will lead some to faith and true life.

ORGANIZATION

Throughout the current work the author will consider several background issues important to any study of 2 Peter. In order to examine texts in 2 Peter exegetically and expositionally, one must understand certain issues. At present, a myriad of critical studies of authorship exist, as identified by Thomas Schreiner.[9] Richard Bauckham writes, "New Testament scholars are now nearly unanimous in the opinion that at least one New Testament letter, 2

---

[8] Martin and Davids, *Dictionary of the Later New Testament*, s.vv. "John, Letters of, 2.2.3."

[9] Schreiner, *1, 2 Peter, Jude*, 255–76.

Peter, is pseudepigraphal."[10] Brown and Meier are among those who see 2 Peter's function purely as pseudepigraphal literature aiming to calm a mid-second-century debate.[11] However, M. J. Kruger wrote in favor of traditional Petrine authorship as not only likely, but preferable, citing both external and internal evidence.[12] Kruger's groundbreaking article brought the author of this book to assume traditional authorship. Due to the narrow scope of this monograph, Petrine authorship will be assumed, as Schreiner also supports, and where applicable the author will indicate interesting factors in the authorship debate. The author will examine the probable date of writing to determine its christological context within the body of the current work. The reader will also find information concerning the setting of 2 Peter in supporting the exegesis and exposition in this study. Last, the current research will investigate and identify the nature of the recipients throughout the body of the work as needed.

Chapter 2 will determine the key christological passages in 2 Peter that pertain specifically to the divinity of Jesus. First, the chapter examines the titles that refer to Jesus as deity. Next, an examination of subsequent references to Jesus' divinity will take place. Then, the study will focus on those passages that refer to Jesus' divinity by way of divine attributes. Also, attention will be given to certain indirect references present in the epistle, which inform the reader about Jesus' divinity. Exegesis of each key Greek verse will be provided as the basis for the exposition. An English translation of each key Greek text will also be provided. The author will consider exegetical and text critical issues that appear concerning the divinity of Jesus found in 2 Peter 1:2; 2:11, 20. Finally, readers will find a summary of the findings of the christological understanding of Jesus' divinity in 2 Peter and how it relates to Petrine Christology elsewhere in the New Testament. This summation will contribute to the conclusion in chapter 4.

Chapter 3 will explore the Christology of the uniqueness of Christ in comparison with the distinct nature of God the Father, as the author of 2 Peter presents it. First, the writer will focus on Jesus' divine Sonship. This is the most important reference to Jesus' uniqueness in the epistle. Second, the author will focus on references that position God the Father as distinct from the Son. Specifically, the study will focus on Peter's understanding of the distinct role of the Son as he emphasizes the role of the Father as Preeminent Author, Magistrate, and Deliverer. The author will give special consideration to text-critical issues that appear concerning the distinctness

---

10 Bauckham, "Pseudo-Apostolic Letters," 469.

11 Brown and Meier, *Antioch and Rome*, 210.

12 Kruger, "Authenticity of 2 Peter."

of Jesus from God the Father found in 2 Peter 1:17, 21, as well as any verses that impact the christological discussion. Third, the author will summarize the findings of Jesus' distinctiveness in 2 Peter and its relationship to Petrine Christology elsewhere in the New Testament.

Chapter 4 will conclude the current work. This chapter will present the implications of the Christology of 2 Peter. This conclusion will provide a basis for a much broader submission of conclusions to the overall understanding of a Petrine Christology, specifically concerning Christ's divinity and distinctiveness from God the Father. This section will determine whether similarities between the broader Petrine Christology and that of 2 Peter exist. This section will conclude with the contribution of the current monograph toward a comprehensive Petrine Christology.

2

Jesus' Divinity in 2 Peter

In 2 Peter, the author emphasizes the divinity of Jesus in no less than three broad categories. First, Peter employed specific titles that clearly point to Jesus' divinity. Second, Peter cataloged a variety of divine attributes that he reserved for Jesus. Third, Peter also constructed particular references that indirectly point to Jesus' divinity. This chapter will examine the language in each of these specific categories and the manner in which it exhibits Peter's christological emphasis.

TITLES OF JESUS' DIVINITY

Peter did not leave the decision to the reader to decide whether or not Jesus is divine. In a variety of instances, Peter routinely used four explicit titles to refer to Jesus' divinity. The author will inspect and explicate each of these occurrences. Peter H. Davids described the titles found in 2 Peter, and he argued that these were titles that directly applied to Jesus to present him "in contrast to the ruling emperor." He wrote, "[W]e recognize 'Jesus the Anointed One' or 'Jesus the Messiah' as a title identifying Jesus of Nazareth as God's promised ruler, and . . . 'Savior' as a title of a ruler is not only appropriate in the ancient world but also appears 24 times in the New Testament (5 times in 2 Peter)."[1] Concerning direct designations of deity, "For God or Jesus, the title 'our God' applied directly to Jesus is either an early textual

---

1 Davids, *Theology of James, Peter, and Jude*, 211.

corruption or else among the highest Christology of the New Testament."[2] Throughout the letter, Peter offered clear titles, descriptors, and references to Jesus' divinity. Peter began in the opening verses of his letter with a clear designation to the deity, θεοῦ ἡμῶν (our God). According to Davids, Peter wanted to say, "Here, [Jesus] is the divinely appointed King to whom such titles really belong. This is the King who has granted them allegiance to his rule and who is the main actor of this letter in the opening exhortation that continues the salutation."[3]

Jesus as God

The first title of divinity Peter attributed to Jesus is θεός (God). Peter used this word twice in the opening two verses of the epistle. This is the only time in the epistle where the word θεός (God) occurs specifically, but Peter clearly set the tone for the rest of the letter as he used this title two times before expanding the rest of the contents to his audience.[4]

Exegetical Exposition of 2 Peter 1:1–2

> 2 Peter 1:1-2: Συμεὼν Πέτρος δοῦλος καὶ ἀπόστολος Ἰησοῦ Χριστοῦ τοῖς ἰσότιμον ἡμῖν λαχοῦσιν πίστιν ἐν δικαιοσύνῃ τοῦ θεοῦ ἡμῶν καὶ σωτῆρος Ἰησοῦ Χριστοῦ, χάρις ὑμῖν καὶ εἰρήνη πληθυνθείη ἐν ἐπιγνώσει τοῦ θεοῦ καὶ Ἰησοῦ τοῦ κυρίου ἡμῶν.[5]
>
> Simeon Peter, servant and apostle of Jesus Christ, to the ones who received our same faith in the righteousness of our God and Savior, Jesus Christ. Grace and peace be multiplied to you in the full knowledge of God and of Jesus our Lord.[6]

Peter began the epistle by immediately drawing attention to Jesus and stating his allegiance and apostleship as being of Ἰησοῦ Χριστοῦ (of Jesus Christ). In the same sentence, he ended by referring to Jesus a second time with the clear title τοῦ θεοῦ ἡμῶν (of our God). Craig Keener wrote that Peter's use of the title τοῦ θεοῦ ἡμῶν καὶ σωτῆρος Ἰησοῦ Χριστοῦ (of our

---

2 Davids, *Theology of James, Peter, and Jude*, 211.

3 Davids, *Theology of James, Peter, and Jude*, 211.

4 Carson, *New Bible Commentary*, 1389.

5 The Greek text comes from Aland, Black, and Metzger's *Greek New Testament*, 4th ed., unless otherwise noted.

6 All English translations of the Greek text are the author's, unless otherwise noted.

God and Savior Jesus Christ) is a "clear statement of his divinity and would have offended most Jewish readers who were not Christians."[7] Not everyone agrees that τοῦ θεοῦ ἡμῶν (of our God) and σωτῆρος (Savior) both refer to Ἰησοῦ Χριστοῦ (Jesus Christ).[8] Richard J. Bauckham wrote, "Some scholars ... think the phrase intends to distinguish God and Jesus (Plumptre, Mayor, Windisch, and Käsemann), but a large majority think that θεοῦ ('God') is here used of Jesus. Elsewhere in the letter the writer uses the similarly constructed phrase."[9] However, Keener's view is preferable. Bauckham also held ultimately that scholars should understand the phrase as describing Jesus.

Davids strongly claimed that "2 Peter starts out with what is arguably the highest expressed Christology in the New Testament, a statement in which Jesus is explicitly called 'God' as well as 'Savior.'"[10] Thomas Schreiner explained that in 1:1 "when two singular nouns, which are not proper nouns, fall under the same article, they refer to the same entity. The phrase used here fits every part of this definition. If Peter wanted to distinguish Jesus Christ from the Father, he would have inserted an article before the noun Savior."[11] The genitive modifier ἡμῶν (our) is also singular, lending weight to Keener's position. Thus, Peter did not make a distinction between the Father and the Son in this instance. Rather, he attributed θεός (God) undoubtedly to Ἰησοῦ Χριστοῦ (Jesus Christ).

The title θεός (God) for Peter most definitely carried with it the meaning of the monotheistic God of Israel.[12] In this definition of θεός (God), Peter certainly included Jesus of Nazareth, as described. Peter used θεός (God) seven times in this epistle (2 Pet 1:1, 2, 17, 21; 2:4; 3:5, 12), but 1:1 is the single occurrence where the title refers to Jesus. While Peter pointed to the deity of Christ in other places, which the author of this monograph will examine, this proves to be a very important instance when Peter used θεός (God) to point to the deity of Christ in a very direct manner.[13] Davids noted that the Codex Sinaiticus includes "our Lord and Savior" instead of "God." He argued that the Granville-Sharp rule demands the translator view 1:1 as referring to one person, writing, "[W]e have two nouns ('God' and 'Savior,' neither of them a proper name) joined by καί with an article before the first

---

7 Keener, *IVP Bible Background Commentary*, loc. cit. "2 Peter 1:1–2."
8 See Neyrey, *2 Peter, Jude*, 147–48.
9 Bauckham, *Jude, 2 Peter*, 168.
10 Davids, *Theology of James, Peter, and Jude*, 210.
11 Schreiner, *1, 2 Peter, Jude*, 286–87.
12 Martin and Davids, *Dictionary of the Later New Testament*, s.v. "God."
13 Martin and Davids, *Dictionary of the Later New Testament*, s.vv. "God: 2 Peter and Jude."

noun ('God') but without the article being repeated before the second noun ('Savior'). Unity is further underlined by an adjective ('our') that describes both nouns but is positioned after the first noun and before καί."[14] In response to those who view this passage as espousing modalism, Schreiner added that many texts in 2 Peter and in the New Testament clearly refer to Jesus as God (John 1:1,18; 20:28; Rom 9:5; Titus 2:13; Heb 1:8), saying, ". . . the intention is never to teach a form of modalism. To deny such a reading here would be to violate the clear sense of the grammar."[15]

For some, the style and supposed date of composition make it difficult to believe that the apostle Peter could have written such complex christological statements at such an early date. Robert G. Bratcher described the difficulty between the style of 1 and 2 Peter. He noted the author's use of Συμεών (Simeon), the Hebraic variant of Simon, as evidence that the letter may have had a different author other than the apostle Peter. He described the competing views of authorship:

> (1) Some scholars believe that the apostle Peter wrote both letters, and that the different styles of the two are explained by the role that Silas had in writing 1 Peter (see 5:12), while the apostle himself wrote 2 Peter. Some believe that 2 Peter was written before 1 Peter. (2) Others believe the apostle wrote 1 Peter but not 2 Peter. 2 Peter was written in the apostle's name by a follower of his, after Peter's death. Dates proposed for this letter range from 95 to 150 A.D. (3) Still others believe both letters were written by a follower of the apostle sometime in the first half of the second century A.D.[16]

Peter also stated χάρις ὑμῖν καὶ εἰρήνη πληθυνθείη (Grace and peace be multiplied to you), which, interestingly, Bratcher pointed out are both kinds of blessings that God grants people in the New Testament. "Grace stands for his love, manifested to all through Jesus Christ, and peace is spiritual well-being, also regarded as God's gift; it may be represented by 'spiritual strength' (see 1 Peter 1.2)."[17] Verse 2 also highlights the deity of Christ subtly by giving or desiring for readers what only God, τοῦ θεοῦ ἡμῶν καὶ σωτῆρος Ἰησοῦ Χριστοῦ (of our God and Savior, Jesus Christ), can give truly. Clearly and significantly, Peter attributed the title θεός (God) to Jesus.

---

14 Davids, *Theology of James, Peter, and Jude*, 210.
15 Schreiner, *1, 2 Peter, Jude*, 287.
16 Bratcher, *Translator's Guide*, 2.
17 Bratcher, *Translator's Guide*, 134.

Jesus as Lord

Second, Peter also described Jesus as κυρίος (Lord). Peter did not appear to have any problem giving Jesus the title κύριος (Lord). Larry Helyer noted that "along with the other New Testament writers, [Peter] identifies Jesus with the exalted Yahweh of the Old Testament, most often translated as 'LORD' in English versions."[18] While κύριος (Lord) has a range of attribution, it is clear from the following texts that it connects itself to the deity of Christ.

Exegetical Exposition of 2 Peter 1:2, 8, 11, 14, 16; 2:20; 3:2, 18

> 2 Peter 1:2: χάρις ὑμῖν καὶ εἰρήνη πληθυνθείη ἐν ἐπιγνώσει τοῦ θεοῦ καὶ Ἰησοῦ τοῦ κυρίου ἡμῶν.
>
> Grace and peace be multiplied to you in the full knowledge of God and of Jesus our Lord.

Just as τοῦ θεοῦ ἡμῶν (of our God) in 1:1 proves itself as a clear reference to the deity of Christ, the prepositional phrases in 2:2, ἐν ἐπιγνώσει τοῦ θεοῦ καὶ Ἰησοῦ τοῦ κυρίου ἡμῶν (in the knowledge of God and of Jesus our Lord), connect θεοῦ (of God) with Ἰησοῦ (of Jesus) with the conjunction καὶ (and). Ἰησοῦ (of Jesus) is modified by the genitive of appellation, τοῦ κυρίου ἡμῶν (of our Lord), connecting Jesus not only to divinity but also to the title of Lord. Robert L. Webb and Duane F. Watson spoke to the numbness that one often feels in today's society when reading the beginning of New Testament letters when the title Lord is found and the lack of understanding concerning the status and significance that comes with the title. They wrote, "By highlighting Jesus and God, Peter lucidly establishes a tone for the instructions that follow. Without question, the word Peter presents to his auditors revolves around Jesus and God."[19] The background of the title κύριος (lord) is very important for a student of the New Testament. Otherwise, like Webb and Watson argued, one may overlook the title as a simple name and miss the significance of its usage to its original audience.

The Hellenistic world before Christ rarely used the title κύριος (lord) to refer to leaders, such as Alexander the Great or Phillip of Macedonia. In the early Hellenistic period, pagan and Greek gods also did not carry the title κύριος (lord). This is significant because the Septuagint (LXX) is the

---

18 Helyer, *Life and Witness of Peter*, 220.
19 Webb and Watson, *Reading Second Peter*, 163.

first known document to employ κύριος (lord) to refer to a deity.[20] Control of someone or something in itself is also not central to the definition of κύριος (lord). In the first century, the noun κύριος (lord) denoted legal ownership over a subject, child, or wife. This was true specifically in Rabbinic Judaism.[21]

In this instance, Peter recognized the legal ownership of Jesus over all those who follow him specifically and the entire universe generally. Peter did not separate Jesus' lordship from his deity. In this instance it signifies and stands for Jesus' deity. Second Peter employs κύριος (Lord) fourteen times. In eight of these instances it is clear that Peter used κύριος (Lord) as a title of a ruler. According to Davids, it "is possible that in all fourteen Jesus is the one indicated" as ruler.[22]

This is significant, as Callan pointed out, because Lord is used more as a title for Jesus in the New Testament than any other word but one. It is interestingly not used at all in Titus or 1–3 John. The Gospels themselves are full of references to Jesus as κύριος (Lord). Callan wrote, "This reflects the later faith of his followers that Jesus is Lord. It seems quite likely that Jesus was called Lord during his lifetime. In the Gospels, Jesus is called Lord by those who are asking for his help and by his disciples. It seems entirely likely that both of these groups would acknowledge his authority by calling him Lord."[23]

This was a term that was commonplace in the Roman Empire. Hearers immediately would have made a connection to Caesar, who also was named κύριος (lord) by the imperial Roman cult. Helyer wrote, "How hollow this [statement of the Roman cult] sounds in comparison with the claims for Jesus the Messiah. With the apostle Paul, Peter affirms that 'Jesus is Lord' (Rom. 10:9)."[24]

Like with Caesar, whom Romans not only worshipped, but to whom all obedience was due as subjugates to his empire, so too this title must have communicated a parallel to the original recipients of this letter within the Roman Empire concerning Jesus. J. D. Charles maintained that Peter intended to pull the reader into the parallel of the Roman and Hellenistic society by employing words like κύριος (lord) in order to contextualize truths about the Christian faith to Hellenistic recipients. Therefore, when

20 Kittel, Friedrich, and Bromiley, *Theological Dictionary*, s.vv. "Κύριος, Κυρία, Κυριακός, Κυριότης, Κυριεύω, Κατακυριεύω."

21 Kittel, Friedrich, and Bromiley, *Theological Dictionary*, s.vv. "Κύριος, Κυρία, Κυριακός, Κυριότης, Κυριεύω, Κατακυριεύω."

22 Davids, *Theology of James, Peter, and Jude*, 234.

23 Callan, *Origins of Christian Faith*, 47.

24 Helyer, *Life and Witness of Peter*, 145.

Peter encouraged his listeners to live pious lives, he did so with the authority of the κύριος (Lord), which carried with it a serious level of commitment, duty, and "one that is consonant with their profession of faith (1:10). The contours of this lifestyle point to a moral progression for which the believer, based on prior knowledge, is ultimately held accountable."[25]

> 2 Peter 1:8: ταῦτα γὰρ ὑμῖν ὑπάρχοντα καὶ πλεονάζοντα οὐκ ἀργοὺς οὐδὲ ἀκάρπους καθίστησιν εἰς τὴν τοῦ κυρίου ἡμῶν Ἰησοῦ Χριστοῦ ἐπίγνωσιν.
>
> For if these are belonging to you and increasing, they make you neither useless nor unfruitful, in the knowledge of our Lord Jesus Christ.

Peter employed the verb ὑπάρχοντα (belonging to), which Louw and Nida suggested means "to exist, particularly in relation to ownership, 'to exist, to belong to.'"[26] Peter implied that by possessing or owning the qualities mentioned in 1:7 one is εἰς τὴν τοῦ κυρίου ἡμῶν Ἰησοῦ Χριστοῦ ἐπίγνωσιν (in the knowledge of our Lord Jesus Christ). Being in the ἐπίγνωσις (knowledge) of κυρίου ἡμῶν (our Lord) again makes the connection to ownership and authority. Again, Peter connected ἐπίγνωσις (knowledge) here in 1:8 with 1:2, ἐν ἐπιγνώσει τοῦ θεοῦ καὶ Ἰησοῦ τοῦ κυρίου ἡμῶν (in the knowledge of our Lord Jesus Christ), where the deity of Jesus so clearly shone. Here as well Ἰησοῦ τοῦ κυρίου ἡμῶν (of Jesus our Lord) harkens back to 1:1, τοῦ θεοῦ ἡμῶν καὶ σωτῆρος Ἰησοῦ Χριστοῦ (of our God and Savior, Jesus Christ). In 1:8, the construction τοῦ + genitive noun + ἡμῶν replaces θεοῦ (God) with κυρίου (Lord). Clearly, in the context of the first eight verses, the original readers would have recognized this and without a doubt would have connected not only θεός (God) with Jesus, but also to κύριος (Lord), the Septuagint's clear descriptor for Yahweh and Adonai.[27]

> 2 Peter 1:11: οὕτως γὰρ πλουσίως ἐπιχορηγηθήσεται ὑμῖν ἡ εἴσοδος εἰς τὴν αἰώνιον βασιλείαν τοῦ κυρίου ἡμῶν καὶ σωτῆρος Ἰησοῦ Χριστοῦ.
>
> For in this way entrance will be abundantly supplied to you into the eternal kingdom of our Lord and Savior Jesus Christ.

1:11 begins with an emphatic placement of πλουσίως ἐπιχορηγηθήσεται ὑμῖν (will be abundantly supplied to you). This signaled to the reader the

---

25 Charles, "Language and Logic of Virtue, 73.
26 Louw and Nida, *Greek-English Lexicon*, 157.
27 Kittel, Friedrich, and Bromiley, *Theological Dictionary*, s.vv. "Κύριος, Κυρία, Κυριακός, Κυριότης, Κυριεύω, Κατακυριεύω."

positivity with which Peter wrote. While themes of judgment and warning arose in connection with the false teachers, he joyfully expressed the blessings available because of the gospel. With πλουσίως ἐπιχορηγηθήσεται ὑμῖν (will be abundantly supplied to you) emphasized as beginning in the third position, Peter emphasized the grace that gave access, here ἡ εἴσοδος (entrance), into and eternal kingdom, and by inference, eternal life. This begs the question, who is the king of τὴν αἰώνιον βασιλείαν (the eternal kingdom), or to whom does it belong? Who is able to grant access, εἴσοδος (entrance), into this kingdom? Peter used a double emphasis by not only beginning with πλουσίως ἐπιχορηγηθήσεται ὑμῖν (will be abundantly supplied to you) in an emphatic position, but placing the name and title of the owner at the end of the thought, as to answer the questions that the reader had when beginning the thought τοῦ κυρίου ἡμῶν καὶ σωτῆρος Ἰησοῦ Χριστοῦ (of our Lord and Savior Jesus Christ) in an appositional clause. Again, Peter followed 1:8, and concerning the grammatical construction τοῦ + genitive noun + ἡμῶν, he replaced θεοῦ (God) with κυρίου . . . Ἰησοῦ Χριστοῦ (Lord . . . Jesus Christ). The Lord, therefore, is the one who is the king of this eternal kingdom. In this context of ancient peoples, the king had absolute authority. Therefore, Peter's use of κύριος (Lord) here denoted a king with absolute eternal divine authority. No kingdom exists that is older or greater than an eternal one, and therefore no king exists or is older than an eternal one. Only the king of an eternal kingdom can ultimately grant εἴσοδος (entrance) into such a kingdom; for only the Eternal Divine Being could own such a kingdom. The word κύριος (Lord) here denotes much more than a mere signal of respect or allegiance. No other credible reading or interpretation is viable of this clear passage.[28]

> 2 Peter 1:14: . . . εἰδὼς ὅτι ταχινή ἐστιν ἡ ἀπόθεσις τοῦ σκηνώματός μου καθὼς καὶ ὁ κύριος ἡμῶν Ἰησοῦς Χριστὸς ἐδήλωσέν μοι.
>
> . . . knowing that the putting off of my tent is imminent just as indeed our Lord Jesus Christ has indicated to me.

The construction changes in this verse from τοῦ + genitive noun + ἡμῶν to simply ὁ κύριος ἡμῶν (our Lord). However, Peter's assertion in this text is that ὁ κύριος ἡμῶν (our Lord) is the same as the one from 1:1, 8 and 11. The readers are charged not only to understand this as coming from Peter, but they should also understand this encouragement to press on living in the qualities and virtues referenced in 1:12 and the position reinforced in 1:13 as being from Jesus, entitled ὁ κύριος ἡμῶν (our Lord). The usage of κύριος (Lord) parallels the kind of authority by which Jesus' followers

---

28 Lukaszewski and Dubis, *Expansions and Annotations*, loc. cit. "2 Peter 1:11."

knew him in the Gospels and in Acts. The New Testament places Peter at the great commission and ascension of Jesus, where he invoked this type of authority, which ὁ κύριος (the Lord) carried with it. In Matthew 28:18, Jesus cited his authority, and it drove his followers to action: "And Jesus came and said to them, 'All authority in heaven and on earth has been given to me. Go therefore and make disciples of all nations, baptizing them in the name of the Father and of the Son and of the Holy Spirit'" (ESV). An intimate connection subsists between the lordship, and thus authority and ownership, of Jesus, due to his divinity and action. Peter used the name of Jesus in 1:14 with the title ὁ κύριος (the Lord), using ἡμῶν (our), as a reminder that Jesus is not just the Lord of the apostles, but he is the Lord of all. The emphatic conjunction καθὼς καὶ (just as indeed) precedes he who revealed (ἐδήλωσέν) to the author this material ὁ κύριος ἡμῶν (our Lord).[29] This incontestably strengthened Peter's reminder with authority not of his own. The aide-mémoire of 1:13 then is from God himself.

> 2 Peter 1:16: Οὐ γὰρ σεσοφισμένοις μύθοις ἐξακολουθήσαντες ἐγνωρίσαμεν ὑμῖν τὴν τοῦ κυρίου ἡμῶν Ἰησοῦ Χριστοῦ δύναμιν καὶ παρουσίαν ἀλλ' ἐπόπται γενηθέντες τῆς ἐκείνου μεγαλειότητος.
>
> For we did not cleverly concoct myths when we made known to you the power and coming of our Lord Jesus Christ, but we became eyewitnesses of His majesty.

Rudolph Pesch believed that a Petrine school existed and had developed in Rome, which sought not only to connect to Romans but also to connect to Peter's Jewish roots, as 1:1 gave evidence, Συμεὼν Πέτρος καὶ ἀπόστολος Ἰησοῦ Χριστοῦ (Simeon Peter and apostle of Jesus Christ). Peter used the Hebraic form of his name here again to draw attention to his origins. For it was in Galilee where, according to the Gospel accounts, he first met Jesus. He sought to tie his origins in the letter with the fact that he was one of the eyewitnesses (ἐπόπται).[30] It is not necessary to assume a Petrine school based upon the connections the author made here. Quite naturally, an aged Peter would have drawn upon his own reputation, which undoubtedly by this point had grown to a place of honor and respect within the local church in Rome, where he penned this brief, and across the Christian circles of the Roman Empire. Peter used apostolic authority, founded by the authority of the Lord Jesus, in order to defend himself and the churches from the false teachers mentioned in this epistle.[31]

---

29 Lukaszewski, *Glossary*, s.vv. "emphatic conjunction."
30 Pesch, *Biblischen Grundlagen*, 53.
31 Pesch, *Biblischen Grundlagen*, 53.

It is with a great authority once again that Peter described Jesus as κυρίου ἡμῶν (our Lord) in 1:16. With all of Peter's authority from Galilee to Rome, he invoked the truth of the promise in this verse concerning the power (δύναμιν) and of the Parousia (παρουσίαν) of God (evidenced by the repetitious usage of κυρίου ἡμῶν, our Lord). A common view during ancient Israel and during the first century was that God himself is not able to lie. Numbers 23:19 exclaims, "God is not man, that he should lie, or a son of man, that he should change his mind. Has he said, and will he not do it? Or has he spoken, and will he not fulfill it" (ESV)? 1 Samuel 15:29 records, "And also the Glory of Israel will not lie or have regret, for he is not a man, that he should have regret" (ESV). Peter subtly suggested this in his statement. Further, μεγαλειότητος (majesty) is also connected to God's glory in Luke 9:43.[32] While the author of 1 Samuel declared God as the Glory of Israel, Peter announced the Lord, κύριος, as τῆς ἐκείνου μεγαλειότητος (of his majesty) in 2 Peter 1:16 to link the promises of Jesus exercising κύριος (Lord) with his deity to undergird his trustworthiness.

> 2 Peter 2:20: εἰ γὰρ ἀποφυγόντες τὰ μιάσματα τοῦ κόσμου ἐν ἐπιγνώσει τοῦ κυρίου [ἡμῶν] καὶ σωτῆρος Ἰησοῦ Χριστοῦ, τούτοις δὲ πάλιν ἐμπλακέντες ἡττῶνται, γέγονεν αὐτοῖς τὰ ἔσχατα χείρονα τῶν πρώτων.
>
> For if after they have escaped the defilements of the world by full knowledge of our Lord and Savior Jesus Christ, and they are again entangled, being defeated, the last has become worse than the first to them.

At the height of Peter's agitated discourse, which began in 2:1, he told the false teachers how ridiculous their actions were. First, he mentioned their miraculous deliverance from τὰ μιάσματα τοῦ κόσμου (the defilements of the world). Once they contaminated and shamed the world, but God delivered them from this.[33] Second, he explained that the false teachers only experienced this by ἐπιγνώσει τοῦ κυρίου ἡμῶν (full knowledge of our Lord). George M. Wieland argued that ἐπίγνωσις (full knowledge) is associated with knowledge of the gospel or faith in the gospel in the Pastoral Epistles. He wrote:

> An idiosyncrasy of the three Pastoral Epistles is that the noun ἐπίγνωσις occurs only in the expression ἐπίγνωσις ἀληθείας (1 Tim 2:4; 2 Tim 2:25; 3:7; Titus 1:1), suggesting to Bultmann that, 'the compound ἐπίγνωσις has become almost a technical

---

32 Zodhiates, *Word Study Dictionary*, s.v. "3168."
33 Brannan, *Analytical Lexicon*, s.v. "μίασμα."

term for the decisive knowledge of God which is implied in conversion to the Christian faith.' The construction εἰς ἐπίγνωσιν ἀληθείας ἐλθεῖν suggests a movement into a state of recognition (cf. the perfect participle ἐπεγνωκόσι in 4:3, defining 'the believers' as those who 'have come to recognize the truth'). With ἀλήθεια as its object, this conversion is envisaged through acceptance of the truth taught by Paul (v. 7). Since 1 Timothy also associates salvation with coming to believe in Christ (1:15–16; cf. 4:10), it seems that believing in Christ and recognizing the truth are contiguous if not equivalent concepts. Nonetheless, while recognition of truth must include a 'noetic component,' more is implied than 'the intellectual acceptance of Christianity.' The concept embraces a decisive 'moment of recognition, i.e. of appropriation and practical realization' which shows itself in a life conformed to the truth of the gospel.[34]

In 2 Peter 2:20, based upon this interpretation of ἐπίγνωσις, it is reasonable to suggest that ἐπιγνώσει τοῦ κυρίου ἡμῶν, the "full knowledge (or recognition) of our Lord," refers to the full knowledge of the gospel "of our Lord." D. A. Dunham wrote that "the noun occurs 20 times in the New Testament, 4 of which are in 2 Peter. In every use it indicates a careful and thorough knowledge, not a partial or incorrect one. The object is 'the Lord and Savior.' It is not merely an abstract concept the people know; the Lord Himself is the object of their knowledge!"[35] Peter told the false teachers that it was their recognition of the gospel of the Lord as the object of their knowledge that gave them access to their deliverance from τὰ μιάσματα τοῦ κόσμου (the defilements of the world). This was certainly clear to the original recipients. Callan noted that ἐπιγνώσις, a full recognition or full knowledge, also fits within the soteriological framework of 2 Peter:

> In 1:3 the author says that Jesus' divine power has given them everything pertaining to life and piety through recognition of the one who called them by his own glory and excellence (v. 3), i.e. Jesus. Jesus has done this by first calling them and then having them answer the call by recognizing him as savior. The first verse of 2 Peter says that the readers have received faith from Jesus. Faith is a synonym for recognition of Jesus, specifically, they have received faith equal in honor to that of Peter and others, through the justice of Jesus. The author presupposes that Jesus' death has transferred human beings from enslavement to corruption to his own service. However, this transfer

---

34 Wieland, *Significance of Salvation*, 56.
35 Dunham, "Study of 2 Peter 2:18–22," 43.

does not take effect until it is known to have occurred. Prior to such knowledge, human beings continue to serve their previous master because they do not know they have a new one. For the author of 2 Peter faith, i.e. recognition of Jesus, is absolutely crucial.[36]

Again, Peter employed the title for the divine name and associated the title with Jesus using the τοῦ + genitive noun + ἡμῶν construction, ἐπιγνώσει τοῦ κυρίου ἡμῶν (full knowledge of our Lord). According to Bruce Metzger, the United Bible Societies committee debated the inclusion of ἡμῶν (our). Metzger wrote:

> On the one hand, the variation in position of ἡμῶν (after κυρίου and/or after σωτῆρος) seems to condemn the word as a scribal addition in both instances. On the other hand, the full form of the expression appears to be a favorite of the author (1:11; 3:18), and scribes could occasionally omit elements from the full form—as is shown here by the absence of καὶ σωτῆρος from L 38 309 425 483 629 1881 copbo eth al. On balance it seemed best to include ἡμῶν after κυρίου (following 𝔓72 ℵ A C P Ψ 614 1739 al), but to enclose it within square brackets in order to reflect the weight of the testimony of B K 049 al.[37]

The committee's inclusion is preferable, but the author of the current monograph holds that the weight of the Petrine usage in other verses deem brackets unnecessary. Therefore, the gospel of our God and Savior Jesus Christ himself (τοῦ θεοῦ ἡμῶν καὶ σωτῆρος Ἰησοῦ Χριστοῦ) rescued even people as wretched as the false teachers. Peter's employment of τοῦ κυρίου ἡμῶν (of our Lord) not only connoted Jesus' deity by means of the grammatical construction and use of the Septuagint's appellation of the divine name Yahweh, but again Peter implied the ownership that Jesus, God of the universe, has over those who have fully recognized, accepted, and believed the gospel, ἐπιγνώσει τοῦ κυρίου ἡμῶν (full knowledge of our Lord). This served as a warning to those who had challenged Peter. Not only was their false teaching and antinomian living causing problems within a church or churches, but the false teachers defied their omnipresent, omniscient, omnipotent Master and Owner, Jesus Christ, God himself, who lives, and as implied in 1:16, reckons all of his debts with patience (3:9), yet with surety. Lord, κύριος, continues as a precise Petrine title for Jesus' divinity.

---

36 Callan, "Soteriology of Second Peter," 553.
37 Metzger, *Textual Commentary*, 635–36.

2 Peter 3:2: . . . μνησθῆναι τῶν προειρημένων ῥημάτων ὑπὸ τῶν ἁγίων προφητῶν καὶ τῆς τῶν ἀποστόλων ὑμῶν ἐντολῆς τοῦ κυρίου καὶ σωτῆρος.

. . . that you should remember the words, which were spoken beforehand by the holy prophets and the commandment by your apostles of the Lord and Savior.

The command ἐντολή does not limit itself. Rather, it implies the commands and responses to the gospel. Bratcher noted that ἐντολῆς τοῦ κυρίου καὶ σωτῆρος (commandment by your apostles of the Lord and Savior) is "essentially the gospel message, regarded not only as the Good News of salvation, but also as a way for Christians to live."[38] Interestingly, 3:2 does not focus purely on the command, but Peter gave the command with three qualifiers or motivations concerning authority in order of strength. First, προειρημένων ῥημάτων ὑπὸ τῶν ἁγίων προφητῶν (words, which were spoken beforehand by the holy prophets) signaled the false teachers and those in the churches who considered following or believing them that the teaching and lifestyle of the false teachers was contrary to the prophets. Here, the prophets speak of the Old Testament, and all of its authority. Until a few decades prior to the writing of 2 Peter, the prophets or the Old Testament represented the complete body of Scriptures and authority for faith. Second, καὶ τῆς τῶν ἀποστόλων ὑμῶν ἐντολῆς (and the commandment by your apostles) exercises apostolic authority within the early church. Peter not only spoke of authority that the prophets had hundreds and even thousands of years before him, but of a prophetic authority that he along with the other apostles held. Peter mentioned the Old Testament prophets, since they were already deceased, and then he spoke of himself and the other apostles to strengthen the authority that was present with his original readers. Third, Peter wrote of the greatest authority, ἐντολῆς τοῦ κυρίου καὶ σωτῆρος (commandment of the Lord and Savior). The translators of the English Standard Version translated ἐντολῆς τοῦ κυρίου καὶ σωτῆρος (commandment by your apostles of the Lord and Savior) before καὶ τῆς τῶν ἀποστόλων (and by your apostles) syntactically, probably in order to avoid confusion about the origin of the command. The weakness, however, in placing καὶ τῆς τῶν ἀποστόλων (and by your apostles) after ἐντολῆς τοῦ κυρίου καὶ σωτῆρος (commandment of the Lord and Savior) is that the translators lose the intended authorial escalation. This escalation builds off of the opening phrase, μνησθῆναι τῶν προειρημένων ῥημάτων (that you should remember the words, which were spoken beforehand). With each phrase, the authority increases. Μνησθῆναι (that you should remember) normally implies a

---

38 Bratcher, *Translator's Guide*, 158.

required response.[39] Peter surely intended more than a cognitive exercise, and actually called for repentance, as he made clear is God's desire in 3:9. Peter wanted them to remember through whom the command came, while ending emphatically with the highest of all authorities, God himself, κύριος (Lord), who literally owns their spirituality and existence. Peter evidently intended κυρίου καὶ σωτῆρος (Lord and Savior) to refer to Jesus, whose divinity he made clear in 1:1, θεοῦ ἡμῶν καὶ σωτῆρος Ἰησοῦ Χριστοῦ (our God and Savior, Jesus Christ), and the relationship between Lord and Savior he demonstrated in 2:20, κυρίου ἡμῶν καὶ σωτῆρος Ἰησοῦ Χριστοῦ (our Lord and Savior Jesus Christ).

> 2 Peter 3:18: αὐξάνετε δὲ ἐν χάριτι καὶ γνώσει τοῦ κυρίου ἡμῶν καὶ σωτῆρος Ἰησοῦ Χριστοῦ. αὐτῷ ἡ δόξα καὶ νῦν καὶ εἰς ἡμέραν αἰῶνος. [ἀμήν].
>
> but grow in the grace and knowledge of our Lord and Savior Jesus Christ. To Him the glory both now and to the day of eternity. Amen.

Verse 18 begins with a positive plea from Peter. He urged the readers to grow in grace and knowledge. Interestingly, Peter did not employ ἐπιγνώσις (full knowledge), as he often used to speak of the full recognition of the gospel, as examined previously. He used the prepositional phrase ἐν χάριτι καὶ γνώσει (in the grace and knowledge). This denoted not a full knowledge but rather a general knowledge. Schreiner noted, "Christ could be understood to be the source of both grace and knowledge. Or Jesus Christ could be the source of grace in the first instance and the object of knowledge in the second. The third option is the most likely, that grace is not connected to Jesus Christ in the sentence."[40] Jamieson, Fausset, and Brown wrote alternatively that it is "the grace of which Christ is the author, and the knowledge of which Christ is the object.[41] Schreiner did not disagree in general of the origins of grace, but he saw a specific grammatical tie to Christ in this passage, arguing that grammatically grace and knowledge cannot be a parallel. In a general way the letter connects all grace and knowledge to Jesus Christ, but this verse does not seem to imply grammatically grace and knowledge are flowing out of Christ as its main focus. The word γνῶσις (knowledge) here is important in this distinction.

In 1:5 and 6 Peter used γνῶσις (knowledge) to describe the type of knowledge that provides an understanding of different qualities and virtues

---

39 Swanson, *Dictionary of Biblical Languages*, s.v. "3630."
40 Schreiner, *1, 2 Peter, Jude*, 401.
41 Jamieson, Fausset, et al., *Commentary*, 523.

of a pious Christian. Otherwise, 2 Peter only uses ἐπίγνωσις (full knowledge). Were the words ἐν χάριτι καὶ γνώσει (in the grace and knowledge) a part of a set phraseology in the early church period, or does Peter employ γνώσει (knowledge) here to differentiate this knowledge from a full recognition of the gospel and someone who has experienced spiritual conversion? It is not entirely clear, but Edwin Blum argued that αὐξάνετε ἐν χάριτι καὶ γνώσει (grow in the grace and knowledge) speaks specifically about a post-conversion growth, since one will never know Christ intimately and completely in this life. This γνῶσις (knowledge) then speaks to the goal "to know Christ in a fuller, more intimate way (Philippians 3:10–13; cf. Eph. 1:17)."[42] Alternatively, ἐπίγνωσις (full knowledge) tends to speak of the full recognition of the gospel that has brought conversion.

Again, τοῦ κυρίου ἡμῶν (of our Lord) follows Peter's favored construction τοῦ + genitive noun + ἡμῶν. Peter exhorted the believers to whom he wrote to grow in κυρίου ἡμῶν (our Lord). Prior to the doxology he wrote ending the letter with the same construction used at the beginning of the letter to call attention so clearly to the deity of Jesus. Duane F. Watson and Terrance Callan wrote, "The doxology with which 2 Peter ends probably implies that the author sees Jesus as God. In the New Testament such a doxology is ordinarily reserved for God. Second Peter's use of such a doxology for Jesus probably indicates that the author sees Jesus as divine."[43] Deuteronomy 5:24 states, "Behold, the Lord our God has shown us his glory and greatness, and we have heard his voice out of the midst of the fire. This day we have seen God speak with man, and man still live" (ESV). Again, Exodus 24:16 records, "The glory of the Lord dwelt on Mount Sinai, and the cloud covered it six days. And on the seventh day he called to Moses out of the midst of the cloud" (ESV). For a Jew to ascribe glory, αὐτῷ ἡ δόξα (to him the glory), to a mere man in conjunction with Lord (LXX, κύριος) certainly would have been blasphemous. So, Peter made it no secret that our Lord, κυρίου ἡμῶν (our Lord), is the one who is to receive δόξα (glory). Making this designation, Peter clearly called Jesus divine by using the title κυρίου ἡμῶν (our Lord) in conjunction with the doxology.

Jesus as Savior

Third, Peter described Jesus as σωτήρ (Savior). In no less than five clear instances, Peter ascribed the title σωτήρ (Savior) to Jesus as a designation

---

42 Blum, "Hebrews through Revelation," 289.
43 Watson and Callan, *First and Second Peter*, 219.

for deity.[44] In each of these, Peter linked κύριος (Lord) or θεός (God) with σωτήρ (Savior). Terrance Callan wrote, "The designation of Jesus as Lord is also related to the presentation of Jesus as Savior. This is suggested by Fee['s] linking of the titles 'Lord' and 'Savior' in several passages."[45] While a connection clearly exists, the title Savior on its own right speaks to the divinity of Jesus, which the author of this work will demonstrate below.

Exegetical Exposition of 2 Peter 1:1, 11; 2:20; 3:2, 18

> 2 Peter 1:1: Συμεὼν Πέτρος δοῦλος καὶ ἀπόστολος Ἰησοῦ Χριστοῦ τοῖς ἰσότιμον ἡμῖν λαχοῦσιν πίστιν ἐν δικαιοσύνῃ τοῦ θεοῦ ἡμῶν καὶ σωτῆρος Ἰησοῦ Χριστοῦ.
>
> Simon Peter, servant and apostle of Jesus Christ, to the ones who received our same faith in the righteousness of our God and Savior, Jesus Christ.

In 1:1, in conjunction with Peter's clear statement of his own service/subjugation to and apostleship of Jesus, δοῦλος καὶ ἀπόστολος Ἰησοῦ Χριστοῦ (servant and apostle of Jesus Christ), signifying his position of authority among the Christian community, he immediately turned to an important group-encompassing phrase, τοῖς ἰσότιμον ἡμῖν λαχοῦσιν πίστιν (to the ones who received our same faith). The *Theological Dictionary of the New Testament* stated, "With striking frequency [λαγχάνω] is . . . combined with the word group κλῆρος, κληροῦν. Even where there is no casting of lots, the attainment is not by one's own effort or as a result of one's own exertions, but is like ripe fruit falling into one's lap. This is always to be kept in mind."[46] Peter drew attention to his salvation by grace in the first line of the letter. Interestingly, he wrote ἡμῖν λαχοῦσιν πίστιν (received our faith), including all the hearers with them. He used his apostolic position, but in the same sentence spoke to the undeserving nature of the gospel for himself and his hearers. Although he held a place of authority among the worldwide church, he humbled himself and left no room for the recipients to boast in any superiority they felt they had. Bratcher recorded, "Though the readers had not, like the Apostles, received their faith directly from Jesus Christ, they were not spiritually inferior to the Apostles."[47] On this point, Callan commented, "The Pauline character of the soteriology of 2 Peter is very marked. In view

---

44 Zodhiates, *Word Study Dictionary*, s.v. "4990."
45 Callan, "Soteriology of Second Peter," 549.
46 Kittel, Bromiley, and Friedrich, *Theological Dictionary*, s.v., "Λαγχάνω."
47 Bratcher, *Translator's Guide*, 134.

of the author's claim (in 2 Pet. 3:16) that Paul agrees with what the author has said, this is not surprising."[48] All received the same grace, not by their own works, but by the mercy of God. The *Theological Dictionary of the New Testament* underscores this point concerning the divine origin of faith:

> ... [T]he point of λαγχάνειν is that faith has come to them from God with no co-operation on their part. That faith is the work, not of man, but of God or Christ, is not stated with equal clarity in all parts of the New Testament, but it must be constantly borne in mind. God does not merely give to both Jews and Gentiles the possibility of faith; He effects faith in them. Ephesians 2:8 makes it especially plain that all is of grace and that human merit is completely ruled out. To understand the Pauline ... doctrine of justification it is essential to make it clear that faith is not a new human merit which replaces the merit of works, that it is not a second achievement which takes the place of the first, that it is not something which man has to show, but that justification by faith is an act of divine grace. Faith is not the presupposition of the grace of God. As a divine gift, it is the epitome and demonstration of the grace of God. All is of grace, and yet God is righteous. With men λαγχάνειν cannot be combined with strictly impartial justice. With the God of Christians, however, free choice, which seems to exclude all justice because it takes place contingently, fuses with real righteousness in a unity which is indissoluble, though beyond the capacity of man to grasp.[49]

It is within this context that Peter attributed this act to θεοῦ ἡμῶν (our God). If the sentence ended after θεοῦ ἡμῶν καὶ σωτῆρος (our God and Savior), it would have fit the Old Testament narrative quite well. Isaiah 43:11–12 states, "'I, I am the Lord, and besides me there is no savior. I declared and saved and proclaimed, when there was no strange god among you; and you are my witnesses,' declares the Lord, and I am God" (ESV). Yahweh, κύριος (Lord) in the Septuagint, proclaims that he is the only Savior who exists. In Isaiah 43:10 God says, "Before me no god was formed, nor shall there be any after me" (ESV). Isaiah's prophecy clearly states that there is only one Savior. To ascribe this title to an ordinary man would have been blasphemous. Psalm 3:8 declares, "Salvation belongs to the Lord ..." (ESV). Therefore, in 1:1, when Peter defined θεοῦ ἡμῶν (our God) as τοῦ θεοῦ ἡμῶν καὶ σωτῆρος Ἰησοῦ Χριστοῦ (to our God and Savior, Jesus Christ), he assigned Ἰησοῦ Χριστοῦ (Jesus Christ) the title of σωτῆρος (Savior), which can only refer to

---

48 Callan, "Soteriology of Second Peter," 559.
49 Kittel, Bromiley, and Friedrich, *Theological Dictionary*, s.v. "Λαγχάνω."

God. Bauckham noted, "The . . . title here given to Jesus, σωτήρ ('Savior'), is found only sixteen times as a christological title in the New Testament."[50] He argued that both Judaism and early Christianity used σωτήρ (Savior) to refer to God.[51] Most likely, early Christians adopted this because of their belief in Jesus' deity. For early Christians Jesus alone, who is God, "exercised the divine function of salvation."[52] While Greeks likely also cognitively connected σωτήρ (Savior) to Christ's divinity, the title specifically speaks to those with Jewish roots and historical worldview. Thus, Peter's usage is a significant christological attribution.

In 2 Peter, when the author used his favored construction τοῦ + genitive noun + ἡμῶν when speaking of θεός (God) or κύριος (Lord) in conjunction with σωτήρ (Savior), he intentionally attributed deity to Jesus. As Nienhuis wrote, "2 Peter shifts emphasis away from Jesus' past messianic death to his present mediatory role as power broker of God's salvation. Second Peter therefore refers to the Lord Jesus as 'the Savior' (1:1, 11; 2:20; 3:2, 18) . . . ."[53] Watson and Callan argued that the grammatical paralleled phrases are much more significant. They argued that the full construction is key to understanding Peter's christological compositions. One finds the grammatical construction article + noun + possessive pronoun + καί + noun + noun + noun also in 1:11; 3:18; and 2:20. Interestingly, "In all of these cases, they designate Jesus as Lord and Savior."[54] Paul also employed this construction once (2 Thess 1:12), which represents its only usage in the New Testament other than in 2 Peter. However, Watson and Callan argued that in 2 Thessalonians Paul applied the structure to a distinction of the Father and Son. In 2 Peter this is a special construction chosen by Peter to emphasize the deity of Christ and his role as not only Lord God but as a divine Savior.

> 2 Peter 1:11: οὕτως γὰρ πλουσίως ἐπιχορηγηθήσεται ὑμῖν ἡ εἴσοδος εἰς τὴν αἰώνιον βασιλείαν τοῦ κυρίου ἡμῶν καὶ σωτῆρος Ἰησοῦ Χριστοῦ.
>
> For in this way entrance will be supplied abundantly to you into the eternal kingdom of our Lord and Savior Jesus Christ.

The first key phrase that denotes the activity of salvation is ἐπιχορηγηθήσεται ὑμῖν ἡ εἴσοδος εἰς τὴν αἰώνιον βασιλείαν (will be supplied to you into the eternal kingdom). The word ἐπιχορηγηθήσεται (will be supplied)

---

50 Bauckham, *Jude, 2 Peter*, 169.
51 Bauckham, *Jude, 2 Peter*, 169.
52 Bauckham, *Jude, 2 Peter*, 169.
53 Nienhuis and Wall, *Reading the Epistles*, 151.
54 Watson and Callan, *First and Second Peter*, 161.

Jesus' Divinity in 2 Peter 25

is passive and "signifies that the subject is being acted upon. A verb in the passive voice with God as the stated or implied agent is often referred to as the 'divine passive.'"[55] The entrance into the kingdom of which Peter spoke will be granted or supplied, ἐπιχορηγηθήσεται. The decision implies a clear active agent who supplies access, who is Jesus Christ in this sentence. The entrance is into an eternal kingdom, and the implied owner and guardian of that kingdom is the Lord, the one who secured and is securing salvation, the σωτήρ (Savior). In 1:11 Peter uses σωτῆρος (Savior), a genitive of possession, which signals ownership or possession.[56] Grammatically Peter made it clear that the kingdom belongs to the Lord and Savior Jesus Christ, τὴν αἰώνιον βασιλείαν τοῦ κυρίου ἡμῶν καὶ σωτῆρος Ἰησοῦ Χριστοῦ (the eternal kingdom of our Lord and Savior Jesus Christ). The opening verse of the letter makes it clear that τοῦ κυρίου ἡμῶν καὶ σωτῆρος (of our Lord and Savior) in 1:11 describes θεοῦ ἡμῶν καὶ σωτῆρος Ἰησοῦ Χριστοῦ (our God and Savior, Jesus Christ) in 1:1. Peter offered a well-defined understanding of the divinity of Jesus with his use of σωτήρ (Savior).

> 2 Peter 2:20: εἰ γὰρ ἀποφυγόντες τὰ μιάσματα τοῦ κόσμου ἐν ἐπιγνώσει τοῦ κυρίου [ἡμῶν] καὶ σωτῆρος Ἰησοῦ Χριστοῦ, τούτοις δὲ πάλιν ἐμπλακέντες ἡττῶνται, γέγονεν αὐτοῖς τὰ ἔσχατα χείρονα τῶν πρώτων.
>
> For if after they have escaped the defilements of the world by full knowledge of our Lord and Savior Jesus Christ, and they are again entangled, being defeated, the last has become worse than the first to them.

Textual evidence exists that would suggest those Peter discussed in this verse are not only false teachers, but perhaps new followers of Christ. Concerning ἀποφυγόντες (they have escaped) in this verse, Dunham pointed out that Peter used αποφεύγω (escaping), a verb, in 2:18 and 20, ἐπιγνώσκω (full knowledge), a noun in 2:20, and a verb, ἐπιγινώσκω (having fully known) in 2:21. In addition, Peter employed the descriptor σωτήρ (Savior) in 2:20. He wrote, "Only one other time does this verb appear in the New Testament, and that is in 2 Peter 1:4, where the apostle expressed his desire that the readers escape the corruptions in the world. In classical Greek it meant 'to escape,' or . . . 'to be acquitted.'"[57] The phrase ἀποφυγόντες τὰ μιάσματα τοῦ κόσμου (they have escaped the defilements of the world) could refer to 1) false teachers who were not truly orthodox believers, 2)

---

55 Heiser and Setterholm, *Glossary*, s.v. "passive."
56 Lukaszewski, *Glossary*, s.vv. "genitive of possession."
57 Dunham, "Study of 2 Peter 2:18–22," 42.

new converts, per Dunham, or 3) new converts who taught falsely and/or lived immorally. While Dunham concluded that 2:20 rules out false teachers and emphasizes new believers, no logical reason exists why a combination of the first two options is not possible. The third option explains Peter's emphasis on the role of σωτήρ (Savior) as a title of Jesus and his work saving those who had experienced deliverance from τὰ μιάσματα τοῦ κόσμου (the defilements of the world).

Ernst Käsemann famously criticized 2 Peter because he felt that it lacked clear teaching on justification.[58] However, he apparently overlooked the soteriological themes such as the christological title for Jesus' deity here. Callan said Peter saw Jesus "as having saved his followers from slavery to corruption and defilement, and argues that the readers must continue in this freedom. Jesus' followers accept salvation from him by faith, which is equivalent to recognition of God and/or Jesus. This recognition must continue and develop through a life of virtue. Likewise, faith must lead to virtue."[59]

Thus, τὰ μιάσματα τοῦ κόσμου (the defilements of the world) represent the old life that was changed by the gospel, the επιγνώσις (full knowledge) in 2 Peter. Peter attributed this work of salvation to Jesus, the σωτήρ (Savior). Peter's argument was that his readers should no longer keep living like they once lived, τούτοις δὲ πάλιν ἐμπλακέντες ἡττῶνται (and they are again entangled), but that they should continue in freedom, ἐν ἐπιγνώσει τοῦ κυρίου [ἡμῶν] καὶ σωτῆρος Ἰησοῦ Χριστοῦ (by full knowledge of our Lord and Savior Jesus Christ). Peter called Jesus the Savior in his favorite construction connoting divinity. He implied clearly by the last clause that these new converts, who also struggled with how to live out the gospel and the Christian life, that their current sin, by implication, was worse than their former sin. The reason being, formerly they were without the επιγνώσις (full knowledge) of God, κυρίου [ἡμῶν] καὶ σωτῆρος Ἰησοῦ Χριστοῦ (our Lord and Savior Jesus Christ), and while still sinners they sinned in ignorance. After receiving the ἐπιγνώσις (full knowledge) of God, they knew and believed the gospel, but they did not demonstrate it in their lives practically or in their teaching. Peter chided them since they no longer practiced their sin in ignorance; rather they acted in rebellion ironically against the Savior who delivered (ἀποφυγόντες) them in the first place from τὰ μιάσματα τοῦ κόσμου (the defilements of the world). Peter emphasized here that their sin was not against a mere man, but these new converts had sinned against God, their divine Lord and Savior, who is Jesus Christ. Second Peter 2:20 represents a substantial use of Jesus as Savior, σωτήρ, in association with his deity.

58 Käsemann, "Apologia," 184.
59 Callan, "Soteriology of Second Peter," 554.

2 Peter 3:2: ... μνησθῆναι τῶν προειρημένων ῥημάτων ὑπὸ τῶν ἁγίων προφητῶν καὶ τῆς τῶν ἀποστόλων ὑμῶν ἐντολῆς τοῦ κυρίου καὶ σωτῆρος.

> ... that you should remember the words, which were spoken beforehand by the holy prophets and the commandment by your apostles of the Lord and Savior.

Peter applied the terms Lord and Savior, τοῦ κυρίου καὶ σωτῆρος, using a different construction than the previous examples. Here, specifically σωτῆρος (Savior) has the syntactic force of a genitive of source.[60] This expresses the source of ἐντολῆς (commandment). The authority by which the recipients received the ἐντολῆς (commandment) came from the σωτήρ (Savior). Peter spoke of the ultimate source of authority by which the hearers received the commandment, τοῦ κυρίου καὶ σωτῆρος (of the Lord and Savior), which grammatically described one person, not two people. The author of this book already showed evidence that Peter employed κύριος (Lord) as a divine title, and in 3:2 σωτήρ (Savior) clearly described the same divine person. The opening (1:1–2) made quite clear that the divine person whom Peter described is Jesus Christ.

Peter probably chose Lord and Savior not only as a reference to the many Old Testament passages that speak of God this way, but also to compliment the force of the lordship of Christ with mercy. Jesus is not the mere human master, as a common lord was to a slave with pure authority, but he has an interest in those over whom he himself lords. The title σωτήρ (Savior) in this verse signifies his compassion for those whom he has purchased and who follow him. If one holds that 1 Peter preceded the composition of 2 Peter, this theme fits quite nicely.

Concerning Jesus' mercy, 1 Peter 1:3–5 records: "According to his great mercy, he has caused us to be born again to a living hope through the resurrection of Jesus Christ from the dead, to an inheritance that is imperishable, undefiled, and unfading, kept in heaven for you, who by God's power are being guarded through faith for a salvation ready to be revealed in the last time" (ESV). The readers likely already had read this opening passage. In other words, as an apostle on behalf of God, Peter reminded the readers that Jesus, the God who demands the readers to follow this command, made this command from a position of understanding, compassion, and as one who gave his life for those whom he loves. The Holman New Testament Commentary noted that "the 'command' refers to the moral demands of the Christian faith, primarily Jesus' command of love reaffirmed by the apostles."[61] Peter

---

60 Lukaszewski and Dubis, *Expansions and Annotations*, loc. cit. "2 Peter 3:2."
61 Walls and Anders, *1 and 2 Peter*, 140.

emphasized with the use of the title σωτήρ (Savior) that God himself gave this command through his prophets and apostles, while having made the ultimate sacrifice so that his followers can live in freedom and follow in his commands. While subtle, this was emphatically intentional. As Peter sought to express a high Christology, he also wrote in an equally fitting style. His high style fit with the high authority with which he wrote. Andrew Chester and Ralph P. Martin underscored the beauty and intentionality of the epistle while specifically noting the planned and intentional nature of 3:2:

> The author's style is carefully crafted, with rhetorical devices such as alliteration (2:12; 2:5) and assonance (2:15–16 where *paranomia* ['transgression'] rhymes with *paraphronia* ['madness'] and a criss-cross arrangement of words to form a chiasmus (1:12–21; 3:2). The impression given is that of a writer who has access to an artificial dialect of high-sounding words learnt from rhetoricians or books, but used with a certain uneasiness associated with a style and language acquired in later life.[62]

The author's careful use of style and vocabulary demonstrates his high Christology. Second Peter does not appear to be a document thrown together haphazardly in order to win a second-century-AD argument. Rather, this is a carefully thought-out letter that is pregnant with intentionality and meaningfulness. With purpose, 2 Peter demonstrates the emphasis of the divine title σωτήρ (Savior) in conjunction with κύριος (Lord) attributed to Jesus Christ.

> 2 Peter 3:18: αὐξάνετε δὲ ἐν χάριτι καὶ γνώσει τοῦ κυρίου ἡμῶν καὶ σωτῆρος Ἰησοῦ Χριστοῦ. αὐτῷ ἡ δόξα καὶ νῦν καὶ εἰς ἡμέραν αἰῶνος. [ἀμήν].
>
> but grow in the grace and knowledge of our Lord and Savior Jesus Christ. To Him the glory both now and to the day of eternity. Amen.

In 3:18 both κυρίου ἡμῶν καὶ σωτῆρος (our Lord and Savior) refer to Jesus Christ. Peter personalized the title with the use of the personal pronoun ἡμῶν (our). Lord and Savior act again together signifying the Old Testament memory of Yahweh, who also described himself this way. However, in this passage Peter described Jesus as the Savior. Just as "Jesus is Lord" sounded provocative to Romans, who declared "Caesar is Lord," so too did the use of "Lord and Savior" in connection to Jesus sound equally provocative to someone familiar with the Septuagint or Hebrew Old Testament.

---

62 Chester and Martin, *Theology of the Letters*, 135.

Glory, δόξα, in the doxology refers clearly to Jesus Christ, also called Lord and Savior in this passage. Remarkably, the high Christology of the doxology at the end of 2 Peter, κυρίου ἡμῶν καὶ σωτῆρος Ἰησοῦ Χριστοῦ (our Lord and Savior Jesus Christ), mirrors the opening address in 1:1, θεοῦ ἡμῶν καὶ σωτῆρος Ἰησοῦ Χριστοῦ (our Lord and Savior Jesus Christ). Bauckham noted, "[This] shows the importance which the Christian attitude of praise and worship toward Christ had for the recognition of this divine status."[63] Furthermore, Bauckham argued that the σωτήρ (Savior) is divine because not only does the doxology describe him with eschatological language, but Peter implied that "glory belongs to Christ not simply 'forever' (the usual word), but throughout the endless day which will dawn when he comes in glory (cf. 1:19)."[64] The doxology of 2 Peter provides one of the strongest examples in the New Testament of σωτήρ (Savior) tied to κύριος (Lord) with an ascription of eternal divine δόξα (glory), ending and accenting one of the most christologically robust New Testament documents.

Jesus as Christ

Fourth, 2 Peter applies the title Χριστός (Christ) to Jesus clearly to denote his deity. The translators of the Septuagint used the word Χριστός (Christ) as a translation of משׁיח (Messiah). Χριστός (Christ) finds its derivation from the verb χρίω, which has the idea of "contact; to smear or rub with oil, i.e. (by implication) to consecrate to an office or religious service:—anoint."[65] New Testament writers often referred to Jesus using the Greek form of the Jewish messianic title, משׁיח (Anointed One or Messiah). Remarkably, no writings or documents outside of the Septuagint, the New Testament, or reliant writings used Χριστός (Christ) when referring to a person.[66]

That the authors of the New Testament agreed that Jesus is the Messiah, Χριστός, helps identify the time in which they wrote, namely, in the period of Second Temple Judaism. Davids reasoned that Second Temple Judaism "expected God to designate or 'anoint' a ruler for his people, usually thought of as a descendant of David on the basis of 2 Samuel 7:12–13."[67] In the opening statement of 2 Peter, the author named the Anointed One Jesus Christ, θεοῦ ἡμῶν καὶ σωτῆρος Ἰησοῦ Χριστοῦ (our God and Savior Jesus Christ). Peter called Jesus Christ or the Anointed One θεός (God). Again,

---

63 Bauckham, *Jude, 2 Peter*, 338.
64 Bauckham, *Jude, 2 Peter*, 338.
65 Strong, *Concise Dictionary*, s.v. "5548."
66 Grundmann, *Theological Dictionary*, s.vv. "Χρίω, Χριστός, Ἀντίχριστος, Χριστιανός."
67 Davids, *Theology of James, Peter, and Jude*, 24.

due to the Granville-Sharp rule, Peter made it clear that there is one being, in essence declaring that "Jesus the Anointed One is God-Savior."[68]

Exegetical Exposition of 2 Peter 1:8, 11, 14, 16; 2:20; 3:18

2 Peter 1:8: ταῦτα γὰρ ὑμῖν ὑπάρχοντα καὶ πλεονάζοντα οὐκ ἀργοὺς οὐδὲ ἀκάρπους καθίστησιν εἰς τὴν τοῦ κυρίου ἡμῶν Ἰησοῦ Χριστοῦ ἐπίγνωσιν.

For if these are belonging to you and increasing, they make you neither useless nor unfruitful, in the knowledge of our Lord Jesus Christ.

Here an intriguing connection exists between ἐπιγνώσις (full knowledge) and Χριστός (Christ) concerning Ἰησοῦς (Jesus). Helyer wrote:

> Peter shows a preference for a compound title bringing together the essential truths about Jesus' identity. Jesus of Nazareth is the promised messiah ('Christ') of Israel's prophetic hope, to be sure, but he is much more than that. By appending the title 'Lord,' Peter transcends a strictly nationalistic conception of the Messiah, since we are now talking about a person who is identified as none other than the sovereign Lord of all creation and history. The majestic strains of Isaiah 40–50 ring in our ears as we contemplate this compound title, 'the Lord Jesus Christ.'[69]

Knowledge, ἐπιγνώσις, then has another strain of depth concerning εἰς τὴν τοῦ κυρίου ἡμῶν Ἰησοῦ Χριστοῦ ἐπίγνωσιν (in the knowledge of our Lord Jesus Christ). Another commentary noted, "Christians should not just possess the virtues in vv. 5–7, but be growing in them. It is possible to have some knowledge of Christ and yet be unproductive."[70] This is the thrust of the idea of knowledge in this passage. A knowledge exists that is not a full knowledge or recognition of who Christ is, whereas a full knowledge and recognition brings growth. One who cognitively understands the truth about Christ will not grow in Christ, but one who knows Jesus personally as Messiah, Χριστός, and Lord, κύριος, will grow to become like him and follow him.

The narrative in the New Testament is that one in the Old Testament experienced salvation when they believed in the coming Messiah, Χριστός.

---

68 Davids, *Theology of James, Peter, and Jude*, 234.
69 Helyer, *Life and Witness of Peter*, 144.
70 Barry, *Faithlife Study Bible*, loc. cit. "2 Peter 1:8."

Those living during the time of Christ, then, would not only have to believe, or fully recognize, Χριστός (Christ) as the Anointed One the Old Testament prophets promised, but they were also charged to fully recognize Jesus, the Χριστός (Christ), as divine. Hence, ἐπίγνωσις (full knowledge) denotes the full recognition of God, the Messiah. The implication is that one must believe that Χριστός (Christ), Jesus, is the Messiah, and that he is divine, as a command from God. Peter presented Χριστός (Christ) as fully divine, yet a part of the Davidic royal line.

> 2 Peter 1:11: οὕτως γὰρ πλουσίως ἐπιχορηγηθήσεται ὑμῖν ἡ εἴσοδος εἰς τὴν αἰώνιον βασιλείαν τοῦ κυρίου ἡμῶν καὶ σωτῆρος Ἰησοῦ Χριστοῦ.
>
> For in this way entrance will be supplied abundantly to you into the eternal kingdom of our Lord and Savior Jesus Christ.

According to Bauckham, the entire section in which 1:8 finds itself makes reference to "Christ's, rather than God's, kingdom. [This] is not very common in early Christian literature. Here it is consistent with the christological focus of the whole section 1:3–11. Of course, the kingdom of Christ is not here distinguished from God's kingdom."[71] Peter described this kingdom of Christ as τὴν αἰώνιον βασιλείαν (the eternal kingdom). Its eternal nature lends weight to Bauckham's contention that Christ here acts as a divine title. Because Christ's kingdom is eternal, it must take an eternal King to rule over it. Also, Χριστός (Christ) carries a salvific hope with it. Jews of the intertestamental period looked forward to a Χριστός (Christ) who would save them from foreign oppression, but they also believed that Χριστός (Christ) would restore the earthly rule of the Davidic line within Israel. So, not only is Χριστός (Christ) the one who saves them, πλουσίως ἐπιχορηγηθήσεται ὑμῖν (will be supplied abundantly to you), but he saves them and restores his rule in an eternal heavenly kingdom, not initially an earthly kingdom. This places his kingdom in the divine realm and not the earthly realm.

Not everyone agrees that 2 Peter employed Χριστός as a salvific title. In the *Theological Dictionary of the New Testament*, Walter Grundmann recorded that in 2 Peter "Χριστός has become part of the proper name of the One through whom salvation has been accomplished; it does not characterise Him as the bringer of salvation."[72] However, it does not exclude the title as referring to a divine being, Jesus. Grundmann described the process of the trial of Jesus before his crucifixion. He underscored the importance

---

71 Bauckham, *Jude, 2 Peter*, 191.
72 Grundmann, *Theological Dictionary*, s.vv. "Χρίω, Χριστός, Ἀντίχριστος, Χριστιανός."

of this event in the formal legal attribution of Jesus as the Messiah. It was Jesus' messiahship that was on trial. Jesus used the opportunity in Mark 15 to accentuate his messianic divinity. Grundmann wrote:

> Pilate adopts the title 'king of the Jews' in his questions at the hearing. Jesus is derided as the king of the Jews (15:18) and this is also the superscription on the cross, 15:26. What is in view is always the Messiah, for this lies behind the title 'king of the Jews.' King of Israel in 15:32 is the more exact designation, cf. also Jn. 1:49. The superscription on the cross has historical significance; it shows that Jesus was crucified as a Messianic pretender. The question of His Messiahship is thus at issue. In the passion story a climax is reached when the high-priest puts the question: σὺ εἶ ὁ χριστός, ὁ υἱὸς τοῦ εὐλογητοῦ; (14:61). In this form the question is shaped by the Christian confession of Jesus as Messiah and Son of God, cf. Mt. 16:16; Jn. 1:49; 20:31. Hence Jesus has to reply in the affirmative. He thus describes Himself as the Son of Man and expounds His Messiahship, which includes divine sonship, in terms of Son of Man Christology. In the question and answer of Mk. 14:61 f. the essential christological predicates are united in Jesus: Messiah, Son of God, and Son of Man. These expound one another. Jesus is the Messiah as the Son of God, and as such He is the Son of Man. New precision is thus given to the meaning of the Messiah by the history of Jesus.[73]

Interestingly, according to Papias, Mark acted as Peter's interpreter, writing down everything that he could remember. Papias described that Peter relayed information about the events in and sayings of Jesus' life in no specific order. Papias wrote, "For of one thing [Mark] took especial care, not to omit anything he had heard, and not to put anything fictitious into the statements."[74] Since Mark was not a disciple of Jesus during his earthly ministry, this was necessary for Mark in the writing of his gospel account to relay the information of an eyewitness. Mark, who apparently traveled with Peter, recorded that which Peter told others as he would travel and preach. The fact that Mark traveled with Peter points to the likelihood that he had a very good tutor and understanding of Christology, including Jesus' role in salvation. Some even believe that 1:15 is a "veiled reference to the Gospel of Mark, where Mark recorded much of Peter's testimony and view of Christ."[75] The latter represents speculation at best.

---

73 Grundmann, *Theological Dictionary*, s.vv. "Χρίω, Χριστός, Ἀντίχριστος, Χριστιανός."
74 Papias, "Fragments of Papias," 154–55.
75 Walls and Anders, *1 and 2 Peter*, 112.

Nevertheless, one's assessment of the date and authorship of 2 Peter surely may carry different readers to a dissimilar interpretation of this passage. Also, one's understanding of the unity of the Scriptures brings diverse presuppositions, which direct one's understanding of the passage in terms of a hermeneutical grid. For instance, if one holds that the author wrote at a late date out of a Petrine school, with a critical view of the unity of the Scriptures, one could easily come to the conclusion that in a later period after the church had already formed itself institutionally Χριστός (Christ) became part of the name of Jesus, but lost its salvific weight. However, if one holds a presupposition of the unity of the Scriptures and that Peter, or with the help of his amanuensis, wrote 2 Peter within the lives of the apostles and early church period, then one would not expect a complete shift of meaning of the title Χριστός (Christ) and all it brings with it. The author of this work holds that this title fits within the christological framework of the Bible and that one simply cannot remove it from its scriptural context. Therefore, an interpreter should view and read Χριστός (Christ) as carrying with it all the nuances of other New Testament passages. While no consensus exists on whether Χριστός (Christ) refers to Jesus' role in salvation, due to one's presuppositional understanding of the Scriptures, one idea remains clear. When Peter referred to Χριστός (Christ) as a title for Jesus, he used it to designate his divinity.

> 2 Peter 1:14: . . . εἰδὼς ὅτι ταχινή ἐστιν ἡ ἀπόθεσις τοῦ σκηνώματός μου καθὼς καὶ ὁ κύριος ἡμῶν Ἰησοῦς Χριστὸς ἐδήλωσέν μοι.
>
> . . . knowing that the putting off of my tent is imminent just as indeed our Lord Jesus Christ has indicated to me.

As the author of the current work once referenced concerning the title κύριος (Lord), ταχινή ἐστιν ἡ ἀπόθεσις τοῦ σκηνώματός μου (the putting off of my tent is imminent) refers most likely to death, although Peter did not specifically say that he would die soon. However, the reference to putting off his tent speaks to his death. Second Peter describes the imminency, here ταχινή (soon), of Peter's death, which was possibly relative, and the first readers may have understood it this way. However, it may point genuinely to a death that Peter himself expected due to external circumstances. Schreiner believes Peter possibly referenced the prophecy John recorded in his Gospel concerning Peter's old age. John 21:18–19 records Jesus telling Peter:

> "Truly, truly, I say to you, when you were young, you used to dress yourself and walk wherever you wanted, but when you are old, you will stretch out your hands, and another will dress you and carry you where you do not want to go." (This he said to

show by what kind of death he was to glorify God.) And after saying this he said to him, "Follow me." (ESV)

According to Schreiner, Peter, who was likely an older man at the time of the composition of 2 Peter, expected with complete faith for this prophecy to take place. He wrote, "Perhaps, if he was in Rome when the letter was written, he could have seen that events were now shaping up that would lead to his death. If the Neronic persecutions had begun, perhaps Peter thought that the end of his life was near with the advent of intense persecution."[76] While 2 Peter does not tell the reader clearly the answer to what the circumstances were surrounding the life and ministry of Peter or definitively whether or not he was in Rome, this line of thought seems plausible. However, it remains in the realm of speculation.

Peter's entire discussion of his death maintains a close connection to the title Χριστός (Christ) in the phrase ὁ κύριος ἡμῶν Ἰησοῦς Χριστὸς ἐδήλωσέν μοι (our Lord Jesus Christ has indicated to me). The messianic title Χριστός (Christ), which in this context likely carries the understanding of salvation with it, may denote that Peter held on to Jesus as Savior Christ, whom he believed prepared a kingdom for him, as he already mentioned in 1:11. Jesus referenced this kingdom in the presence of Peter in John 14, as he stated his divinity and exclusivity. Jesus promised Peter and the disciples that he must leave to prepare a place for all of those who believe in him. Ironically, Jesus told his disciples this directly after prophesying in John 13 that Peter would deny him three times. This instance, due to the prophecy and the promise, likely turned into clear memories for Peter. Consequently, in this passage Peter likely looks into the future not at his own death as much as the salvation that the divine κύριός (Lord) would provide him. As Χριστός (Christ), Peter believed Jesus would come for him at just the right time, not saving his earthly life, but saving him from death to life, while giving the divine Jesus glory in his death.

Marvin Richardson Vincent noted that ἔξοδον (departure) in the following verse, from which the English word for the second book of the Pentateuch, *Exodus*, comes, "is the term used by Luke in his account of the transfiguration."[77] The author of Hebrews also used this word to describe Israel's departure from Egypt. Moses was a type of Messiah for Israel, and therefore this image was likely present for Peter. As for the transfiguration imagery, Moses was present with Elijah for this event, of which Peter also had an eyewitness view. Peter used the words σκηνώματός μου, my tent, to describe his body. This is also the same terminology, τρεῖς σκηνάς (three

---

76 Schreiner, *1, 2, Peter, Jude*, 310.
77 Vincent, *Word Studies*, s.v. "ἔξοδον."

tents), per the Gospel of Mark's account, that Peter used when he felt nervous and did not know what to say on the Mount of Transfiguration. This took place almost directly after Peter's confession of Jesus as the Messiah and the Son of the living God (See Mark 8:29; Matt 16:16). In the context of 2 Peter and in light of the context of other New Testament passages where Peter played a significant role, one uncovers a clear reference in 1:14 to Χριστός (Christ) used as a divine title.

> 2 Peter 1:16: Οὐ γὰρ σεσοφισμένοις μύθοις ἐξακολουθήσαντες ἐγνωρίσαμεν ὑμῖν τὴν τοῦ κυρίου ἡμῶν Ἰησοῦ Χριστοῦ δύναμιν καὶ παρουσίαν ἀλλ' ἐπόπται γενηθέντες τῆς ἐκείνου μεγαλειότητος.
>
> For we did not cleverly concoct myths when we made known to you the power and coming of our Lord Jesus Christ, but we became eyewitnesses of His majesty.

In 1:16 Peter implored his readers to remember not only the power of the Lord, κύριος, but the promise of Parousia, here δύναμιν καὶ παρουσίαν (power and coming), of the Χριοστός (Christ). In the Jewish Old Testament narrative, the people of the earth had waited since the time of the garden of Eden for a Messiah (see Gen 3:15). During the Babylonian captivity, the desire for a Messiah grew. Throughout the Intertestamental Period, under the oppression of multiple foreign powers, this longing developed to a greater extent. When Jesus finally came on the scene in the flesh (see John 1:1), there must have been a feeling of relief from his followers that the wait was finally over. Great anticipation among his followers existed. Peter likely had the events of Acts 1:6–11 in mind when he wrote this in 1:16. Just prior to the ascension of Christ to the right hand of the Father in heaven, one of his followers asked:

> "Lord, will you at this time restore the kingdom to Israel?" He said to them, "It is not for you to know times or seasons that the Father has fixed by his own authority. But you will receive power when the Holy Spirit has come upon you, and you will be my witnesses in Jerusalem and in all Judea and Samaria, and to the end of the earth." And when he had said these things, as they were looking on, he was lifted up, and a cloud took him out of their sight. And while they were gazing into heaven as he went, behold, two men stood by them in white robes, and said, "Men of Galilee, why do you stand looking into heaven? This Jesus, who was taken up from you into heaven, will come in the same way as you saw him go into heaven." (Acts 1:6–11, ESV)

His followers celebrated that the Messiah was finally in Israel, an event that they had anticipated highly. One can imagine the range of emotions they may have felt, as they saw their King, whom they believed to be God and the Messiah in one person, crucified on a cross, only to see him rise from the dead. It is with this background that the followers anxiously asked if Jesus would finally institute his earthly rule. Jesus' response speaks to the δύναμιν καὶ παρουσίαν (power and coming) Peter employed in 1:16. While Luke used a different word than παρουσίαν (coming; in Luke, ἐλεύσεται, will come), essentially the themes of power and Parousia presented themselves clearly. Bratcher clarified that Parousia is special in the New Testament "for the return of Christ at the end of the age, which is commonly spoken of as the Second Coming. The apostolic message about the Lord's return in power was not based on cleverly fashioned legends, but on the firsthand witness of Christ's divine majesty on the Mount of Transfiguration."[78] Jesus pointedly told his followers, and Peter in 1:16 of Jesus, that the Messiah's coming was twofold. First, he came once in the flesh as the Χριστός (Old Testament anticipation) and he rules as κύριος (δύναμιν), and second, he will return as κύριος καὶ Χριστός (δύναμιν καὶ παρουσίαν).

Peter described himself and the other followers as eyewitnesses, ἐπόπται. Peter exhorted that just as some of his readers may have seen God come in the flesh as the Messiah in the person of Jesus, his followers could have confidence that he surely would return, as he stated prior to his ascension. The parallel of the thought flow of Acts 1 is striking. Essentially, Peter told the readers that God had kept his promise once, he ruled currently, and no good reasons existed to question his Parousia or his power. He would return indeed. Just as the timing of the first coming was something only God knew, so the second coming is something only God knows. Furthermore, just as the Old Testament scriptures were not concocted myths, Peter argued at the beginning of 1:16 that neither was the message he received concocted in such a way. In this epistle, Peter sought to fight a battle against false teachers, who accused him of cleverly devising myths.

Some scholars in recent times have also found themselves guilty of such accusations. R. C. Sproul wrote:

> One of the most influential New Testament scholars in the twentieth century was Rudolf Bultmann. He was noted for his program of demythologizing the New Testament. Bultmann created a blitzkrieg in the New Testament world, and for decades New Testament scholars were scrambling to complete the work of removing myth from the text of Scripture. Peter is

---

78 Bratcher, *Translator's Guide*, 141.

saying that the Word of God has already been demythologized. It is not based on myths but on sober, historical reality.[79]

Peter presented Jesus as not only having come, but as coming, and Peter achieved this with the connection of the divine title Χριστός (Christ).

Peter emphasized the majesty of Christ, here τῆς ἐκείνου μεγαλειότητος (of his majesty). *The Expositor's Greek New Testament* connected the majesty of Christ to his divine royalty as the God-ruler of heaven and earth, stating, "Παρουσία occurs frequently in the Papyri as a kind of *terminus technicus* with reference to the visit of the king, or some other official."[80] This language, then, of Χριστός (Christ) also carries clearly that Jesus not only came as an earthly ruler, but he came as ruler of a much greater domain. According to 2 Peter, his domain is an eternal one. This statement of deity comes not only from Peter, but in this pericope's context. God is the one who presents himself as divine Χριστός (Christ). Nienhuis and Wall commented that it "is significant in this regard that 2 Peter's christological confession is vocalized by God (rather than the faith community). The Lord Jesus Christ is known by his apostolic representatives in terms of his 'power and parousia' (1:16) rather than in terms of his obedient suffering and atoning death."[81] Nienhuis and Wall did not mean that Peter did not regard or even mention the redemption provided through Christ (2:11), but that through the apostles God spoke, which he emphasized in 3:2. Since God is the orator, the word is trustworthy, and Christ's Parousia is sure. This is the strongest statement of position, power, and coming action from the divine Christ that Peter could have given. Peter presented himself as a mouthpiece and God as the voice. Peter wrote emphatically to end the pericope, "For no prophecy was ever produced by the will of man, but men spoke from God as they were carried along by the Holy Spirit" (1:21, ESV). Therefore, Peter wrote that the prophecy and statements about the κύριος (Lord), the God-King Χριοστός (Christ), did not come from cleverly concocted μύθοις (myths); rather the prophecy, including statements concerning the Messiah's identity as divine, came from God himself, underscoring the divinity of Jesus in this passage.

2 Peter 2:20: εἰ γὰρ ἀποφυγόντες τὰ μιάσματα τοῦ κόσμου ἐν ἐπιγνώσει τοῦ κυρίου [ἡμῶν] καὶ σωτῆρος Ἰησοῦ Χριστοῦ, τούτοις δὲ πάλιν ἐμπλακέντες ἡττῶνται, γέγονεν αὐτοῖς τὰ ἔσχατα χείρονα τῶν πρώτων.

---

79 Sproul, *1–2 Peter*, 229.
80 Nicoll, *Expositor's Greek New Testament*, loc. cit. "2 Peter 1:16."
81 Nienhuis and Wall, *Reading the Epistles*, 151.

> For if after they have escaped the defilements of the world by full knowledge of our Lord and Savior Jesus Christ, and they are again entangled, being defeated, the last has become worse than the first to them.

As the last word of an appositional clause, the descriptive genitive noun Χριστοῦ (of Christ) acts epexegetically, modifying κύριου (of [our] Lord). While the modern reader may pass quickly over the title Χριστός (Christ) as part of the name of Ἰησοῦς (Jesus), it serves here subtly in a descriptive manner. In 2:20, Χριστοῦ (of Christ) functions as a descriptive title that modifies κύριου (of [our] Lord), which within its context points clearly to Jesus as divine and as the same God of the Old Testament. Χριστοῦ (of Christ) also modifies σωτῆρος (of [our] Savior) epexegetically. The combination is interesting because translators of the Old Testament in the Septuagint used the root word of Χριστός (Christ or Anointed One), χρίω (I anoint), to describe the ones anointed as high priests. However, the Old Testament also used this word to describe others who would act as redeemers of God's people. In the New Testament, Zodhiates also believes that the application of Χριστός (Christ) to the name Ἰησοῦς (Jesus) emphasizes divinity.[82] That Χριστοῦ (of Christ) modifies both κυρίου [ἡμῶν] (of our Lord) and σωτῆρος (of [our] Savior) combines the Old Testament functions of priest and king-redeemer into one individual, Jesus. This resembles that which the writer of Hebrews emphasized, that Jesus is Prophet, Priest, and King (see Heb 1:1-4). Whereas ancient Israel may have expected that different people would fulfill these offices, the New Testament writers brought them together into one person, Jesus.

Isaiah 9:6 was likely in Peter's memory as he combined titles, which states, "For to us a child is born, to us a son is given; and the government shall be upon his shoulder, and his name shall be called Wonderful Counselor, Mighty God, Everlasting Father, Prince of Peace" (ESV). Isaiah's messianic prophecy includes the fact that he will be a Son. Son of God is not only a messianic title itself, but denotes divinity in the New Testament. In Isaiah 9:6 the Son is even called Mighty God. This is one of the strongest passages of support in the Old Testament where one sees a thread of the Messiah's divinity very clearly. Therefore, as a Son of God, the Messiah, he is also God. Peter described the ἐπιγνώσις (full knowledge) of Christ in 2:20, combining his various titles to accentuate Jesus' divinity with the careful use of each title. Isaiah 9:7 combines more of the divine themes: "Of the increase of his government and of peace there will be no end, on the throne of David

---

82 Zodhiates, *Word Study Dictionary*, s.v. "5547."

and over his kingdom to establish it and uphold it with justice and with righteousness from this time forth and forevermore" (ESV).

Jesus also clearly identified himself as the Messiah in quoting Psalm 110:1 in Matthew. Jesus answered a question concerning a similar inquiry of the possibility of the combination of titles such as κύριος (Lord) and Χριστός (Christ) and how the Messiah could be a υἱός (Son). First, Jesus asked the Pharisees a question about whose son the Messiah would be. They answered that the Messiah would be the son of David (Matt 22:42). Jesus then asked the Pharisees, "How is it then that David, in the Spirit, calls him Lord, saying, 'The Lord said to my Lord, "sit at my right hand, until I put your enemies under your feet"'? If then David calls him Lord, how is he his son?" (Matthew 22:43–45, ESV). In this passage, Jesus not only identified himself as the Messiah by his indirect and clever answer to the Pharisees, but he also affirmed the deity of Χριστός (Christ) and his unity with κύριος (Lord). Isaiah also spoke of an eternal kingdom that the Messiah-Son-God would someday rule. Peter's astute readers, who made themselves aware of the Old Testament prophets, likely would have recognized this theme, which began in 1:11 when Peter spoke of ἡ εἴσοδος εἰς τὴν αἰώνιον βασιλείαν τοῦ κυρίου ἡμῶν καὶ σωτῆρος Ἰησοῦ Χριστοῦ (the entrance into the eternal kingdom of our Lord and Savior Jesus Christ). Isaiah wrote that the Messiah will "establish . . . and uphold . . . with justice and with righteousness" (Isa 9:7). If one follows this theme, it is also possible to connect the kingdom of the Messiah in Isaiah with the opening verse of the current epistle, where Peter recorded the connection of Χριστός (Christ) with δικαιοσύνη (righteousness) with the faith of those who will enter the eternal kingdom (ἡμῖν λαχοῦσιν πίστιν ἐν δικαιοσύνῃ τοῦ θεοῦ ἡμῶν καὶ σωτῆρος Ἰησοῦ Χριστοῦ). Nijay K. Gupta even defined Christology specifically as the way it "concentrates on how Jesus fulfills, exercises, and redefines what it means to be the Messiah of Israel."[83] Throughout this epistle, Peter continued to use Χριστός (Christ) subtly yet clearly as a title of Jesus' divinity, and he expressed a high Christology via combined titles as he redefined readers' presuppositions about messiahship, which Jesus' fulfilled.

> 2 Peter 3:18: αὐξάνετε δὲ ἐν χάριτι καὶ γνώσει τοῦ κυρίου ἡμῶν καὶ σωτῆρος Ἰησοῦ Χριστοῦ. αὐτῷ ἡ δόξα καὶ νῦν καὶ εἰς ἡμέραν αἰῶνος. [ἀμήν].
>
> but grow in the grace and knowledge of our Lord and Savior Jesus Christ. To Him the glory both now and to the day of eternity. Amen.

---

83 Barry, *Lexham Bible Dictionary*, s.v. "Christology."

Although certain groups, such as Roman Catholics, sometimes voice prayers to non-deities, this was not a common practice for Jewish believers, such as Peter. On this note, Blum recorded, "For a Jew who has learned the great words in Isaiah 42:8—'I am the Lord; that is my name! I will not give my glory to another'—this doxology is a clear confession of Christ (cf. John 5:23: 'that all may honor the Son just as they honor the Father')."[84] Bratcher reminded translators of the importance of understanding αὐτῷ ἡ δόξα (to him the glory) as a prayer of thanksgiving to Christ. Glory, δόξα, harkens back to the majesty, greatness, and divine power. An exhortation is within the prayer. He suggested the thrust of the verse is "Let us praise Christ for his glory" or "Let us praise and honor Christ."[85] Peter's use of δόξα (glory) as an ascription to Christ reiterated his rich christological emphasis throughout the entire epistle. Bauckham remarked, "The doxology addressed to Christ in 3:18 is consistent with a Christology in which θεός ('God') can be used of Christ."[86] The doxology is remarkable, for it is a clear recognition of the deity of the Messiah, and it clearly designates Jesus throughout the epistle as the one who holds the title Χριστός (Christ).

Concerning Jesus' deity, one must not overlook the connection between κυρίου ἡμῶν (of our Lord) and Χριστός (Christ). In the translation of the Hebrew Old Testament, the translators of the Septuagint used ὁ κύριος (the LORD) in place of the divine name Yahweh. Concerning κύριος (lord) Zodhiates wrote, "In the New Testament, calling upon the name of the Lord Jesus (Acts 9:21 [cf. 9:14; 2:21; 22:16; Rom. 10:13; 1 Cor. 1:2]) was the same language ascribed to those who worshiped the true God of the Old Testament (cf. Gen. 4:26; 12:8; 2 Kgs. 5:11) . . . and Peter posits universal dominion of the same Person—'He is Lord of all' (Acts 10:36)."[87] Therefore, the divine glory that 2 Peter ascribes to Jesus in the doxology clearly applies to the connected title Χριστός (Christ).

ATTRIBUTES OF JESUS' DIVINITY

Just after his grand opening declaration of the deity of Christ with the title θεοῦ ἡμῶν καὶ σωτῆρος Ἰησοῦ Χριστοῦ (our God and Savior Jesus Christ) in 1:1, and once again θεοῦ καὶ Ἰησοῦ τοῦ κυρίου ἡμῶν (God and Jesus our Lord) in 1:2, Peter continued with two important attributes. Peter's high Christology not only included clear titles of his divinity, but it also included

---

84 Blum, "Hebrews through Revelation," 289.
85 Bratcher, *Translator's Guide*, 167.
86 Bauckham, *Jude, 2 Peter*, 168.
87 Zodhiates, *Word Study Dictionary*, s.v. "2962."

many attributes associated with his divinity. It is only logical that 2 Peter, which uses such clear titles to refer to Jesus as a deity, would also attribute and describe him in such a way that includes clear qualities. Specifically, Peter employed hapax legomena in this epistle in two clear instances in reference to Jesus' divinity, divine power, θείας δυνάμεως in 1:3, and divine nature, θείας ... φύσεως in 1:4. Kenneth O. Gungel noted that "Both [1 Peter and 2 Peter] are filled with hapax legomena, words that occur only once in the New Testament, 1 Peter contains 62 and 2 Peter has 54 more, proportionately, than most New Testament books their size."[88] Whether or not they were already in the Christian vocabulary prior to this epistle's composition is unknown. Even though scholars debate the authorship and style of 2 Peter, the fact that both epistles employ such a high number of hapax legomena is striking. This fact heightens the importance of these attributes because they exclusively express Peter's Christology. The author chose these terms specifically to elucidate his views of Christ.

Jesus' Divine Power

The first attribute Peter recognized as belonging to Jesus is divine power, θείας δυνάμεως, in 1:3. Davids viewed this phrase as difficult in terms of grammar. However, he noted that the author's objective came across to the readers in a very well-defined manner.[89] The author's reference to God as θείας δυνάμεως (divine power) is a curious and abnormal locution. One only finds a comparable expression of θείας δυνάμεως (divine power) in Paul's speech on Mars Hill in Acts. Most scholars view this usage, however, as a genuine hapax legomenon. He tied the divine power unswervingly to the gospel. God, who is clearly Jesus (1:1–2), has given the ἐπιγνώσις, a gospel knowledge, by means of his divine power. Since the believers already believed on the gospel, they received access to this divine power in Christ. This ἐπιγνώσις (full knowledge) was the basis for their power and motivation to live godly lives. The recipients lacked nothing for piety. Peter began with an appropriate attribute, which provided encouragement. His encouragement was only possible if Jesus truly is divine, as Peter argued in 1:3.[90]

---

88 Gungel, "2 Peter," 860.
89 Davids, *Theology of James, Peter, and Jude*, 212.
90 Davids, *Theology of James, Peter, and Jude*, 212.

Exegetical Exposition of 2 Peter 1:3

> 2 Peter 1:3: Ὡς πάντα ἡμῖν τῆς θείας δυνάμεως αὐτοῦ τὰ πρὸς ζωὴν καὶ εὐσέβειαν δεδωρημένης διὰ τῆς ἐπιγνώσεως τοῦ καλέσαντος ἡμᾶς ἰδίᾳ δόξῃ καὶ ἀρετῇ.
>
> Because his divine power has granted us everything necessary for life and piety through the full knowledge of him who called us by his own glory and virtue.

The nearest antecedent to αὐτοῦ (his) that modifies θείας δυνάμεως (divine power) is Ἰησοῦ τοῦ κυρίου ἡμῶν (Jesus our Lord) in 1:2. Bauckham wrote that while "it is impossible to be sure . . . whether αὐτοῦ refers to Jesus, . . . [it] is more probable."[91] Bratcher agreed with Bauckham and held that its level of clarity demands that its translation receive careful treatment as to reflect this idea of a divine Jesus. He even suggested the following dynamically equivalent translation: "Jesus Christ has God's power, and he has given it to us."[92] Bauckham warned against such a translation because it suggests that Jesus has a "divine or Godlike power of his own, as though he were a second god."[93] θεῖος (divine) possesses a certain flexibility. Therefore, as Bauckham insisted, it is important that the translator and interpreter convey the clear meaning that Jesus is not a lesser God with a power that is quasi-divine. Rather, he enjoys and occupies the same divinity as God. Bauckham wrote, "It is the same power which will be manifested at the parousia of Christ. (1:16)."[94] However, θείας (divine) should be classified as an attributive adjective, not a predicate adjective, based upon the word order Peter uses.[95] The θείας δυνάμεως (divine power) describes Jesus then as possessing a divine power that is fully his own because he is divine, not because he is similar to God.

In Callan's article on the style of 2 Peter, he explained that Peter wrote in a grand style. During the probable time of composition, writers used this style to emphasize power and they used it intending to impress readers. As Peter exhorted the believers and warned them against false teaching, he used a combination of emotional and rational appeals. His grand style communicated his emotional appeals, while his arguments represented his rational appeals. Callan wrote the following concerning Jesus' divine power,

---

91 Bauckham, *Jude, 2 Peter*, 177.
92 Bratcher, *Translator's Guide*, 135.
93 Watson, and Callan, *First and Second Peter*, 161.
94 Bauckham, *Jude, 2 Peter*, 177.
95 Lukaszewski and Dubis, loc. cit. "2 Peter 1:3."

nature, confirmation of believers' calling, their desire to grow, and their eventual entrance into his eternal kingdom: "We may readily agree that these are indeed powerful and impressive thoughts."[96]

Frederick Danker argued that Peter employed a specific type of Hellenistic decree in order to give honor to the kingship of Jesus. He offered the following as a parallel example: "[One ancient Roman document] introduces a preamble commemorating the birthday of Caesar Augustus: 'Inasmuch as Providence, which ordains everything for our lives, has not only displayed zeal and munificence in the past but has now adorned our lives with perfection itself by bringing us Caesar.'" This type of royal decree indicates that Jesus' divine goodness comes via his divine power.[97] Therefore, not only was the appeal emotional, per Callan, but the emotion that the writing style brings forth is emotional because it was familiar. When speaking of a supreme ruler like Caesar, who many Romans also worshipped, Peter presented Jesus as the object of this type of honor. This surely was scandalous, and provides insight to one of the many reasons Christians underwent persecution during this time period under a totalitarian dictatorial government that sought only its own good and preservation. For Peter to use a style of language only fit for Caesar is yet again an attestation to his reverence for and recognition of Jesus as God.

As a part of the royal honor given only to supreme kings during this period, Peter also used a combination of words, δόξῃ καὶ ἀρετῇ (glory and virtue), that, for the very reason that writers reserved them for rulers, are rare in the New Testament. The only other instance of ἀρετῇ (virtue) in the New Testament is in 1 Peter 2:9. In his impressive and convincing defense of traditional Petrine authorship, M. J. Kruger remarked that "it is important to note that [ἀρετῇ] is rare in the New Testament and in both verses the word is applied to God himself."[98] It is indeed remarkable, and it underscores both Callan and Danker's arguments concerning the style of 2 Peter and its significance in its use of a grand style. The grand style places the date of composition of 2 Peter within the period of its normal usage, which authors reserved for supreme loyalty. Concerning δόξῃ καὶ ἀρετῇ (glory and virtue), in his study on the function of καί (and/even/also) in the New Testament and specifically in 2 Peter, Kermit Titrud wrote that the two words are "closely related in meaning.... Both δόξα and ἀρετή have a wide range of meaning. The juxtaposition of these two lexical items linked

---

96 Callan, "Style of Second Peter," 224.
97 Danker, "2 Peter 1," 67.
98 Kruger, "Authenticity of 2 Peter," 659.

by καί limit their range of meanings to that of denoting divine power."⁹⁹ In his description of the limitation of the exegetical richness of each word in the pair, he also noted that such constructions in the New Testament and specifically in 2 Peter emphasized the object who received the effect of both words. Thus, in 1:3 glory and virtue, δόξῃ καὶ ἀρετῇ, emphasized the divinity of Christ, whose θείας δυνάμεως (divine power) called the believers and supplied ἐπιγνώσις, full knowledge (implying the knowledge of the gospel). Peter richly and clearly expressed his high Christology by means of attribution of θείας δυνάμεως (divine power) to Jesus.

Jesus' Divine Nature

Peter also made clear reference to Jesus' divine nature, θείας . . . φύσεως. One's understanding of the unity of the Scriptures once again will play a role in how one views this passage. Questions have abounded throughout the history of interpretation about what kind of θείας φύσεως (divine nature) believers will actually share in, κοινωνοί. Concerning Ernst Käsemann's statement about 1:4, of which he held that the author of 2 Peter presented a very clear reversion to what he called Hellenistic dualism, James M. Starr understood that Käsemann held that the phrase θείας κοινωνοὶ φύσεως (partakers of divine nature) suggested that the interpreter ". . . can and should escape the material world and our mortal humanity, and take on nothing less than divinity . . . [providing] a clear example of Hellenistic, non-Christian thought insidiously working its way into the New Testament."¹⁰⁰ The questions arise: 1) Is this really an example of Hellenistic dualism? 2) Do other commentators agree with Käsemann's assessment as Starr explained? Even Starr admitted that the "letter's introduction ends with the reader's ultimate hope of entry into Christ's eternal kingdom, which repeats the understanding that sharing in divine nature means incorruptibility."¹⁰¹ Determining what it means to share in the divine nature, θείας κοινωνοὶ φύσεως, is key in understanding what Jesus' nature actually is. The following exegetical exposition will examine θείας κοινωνοὶ φύσεως (partakers of divine nature) in 1:4 and its surrounding context in order to determine what an interpreter may glean about Peter's view of Jesus.

---

99 Titrud, "Function of καί," 259.
100 Starr, "Does 2 Peter Speak of Deification?," 81.
101 Starr, "Does 2 Peter Speak of Deification?," 82.

Exegetical Exposition of 2 Peter 1:4

2 Peter 1:4: δι' ὧν τὰ τίμια καὶ μέγιστα ἡμῖν ἐπαγγέλματα δεδώρηται, ἵνα διὰ τούτων γένησθε θείας κοινωνοὶ φύσεως ἀποφυγόντες τῆς ἐν τῷ κόσμῳ ἐν ἐπιθυμίᾳ φθορᾶς.

By which he has granted us his precious and great promises, so that by them you may become partakers of divine nature having escaped the destruction that is in the world because of desire.

The key christological attributional phrase in 1:4 is γένησθε θείας κοινωνοὶ φύσεως (you may become partakers of divine nature). In order to determine the divine nature in which one has become a partaker, γένησθε θείας κοινωνοὶ φύσεως, the interpreter must first determine which ἐπαγγέλματα (promises) Peter suggested. The introductory words of 1:4, δι' ὧν (by which), act as a continuation of 1:3. The promises, ἐπαγγέλματα, in 1:4 refer to the glory and virtue, δόξῃ καὶ ἀρετῇ, of the divine Christ in 1:3.[102] Both terms act emphatically to accentuate the deity of Christ, by which the gospel came through the ἐπιγνώσις (full knowledge) of God, as the author of the current work discussed in the previous exposition. The perfect middle (deponent) indicative δεδώρηται (he has granted) matches the participle in 1:3. According to Robert James Utley, the implication is that the "deity's divine power has given and continues to give believers all they need both initially (justification) and continually (sanctification) by means of His promises."[103] Therefore, conceptually the ἐπαγγέλματα (promises) refer to justification; this is the knowledge of the gospel through Christ.

Simon J. Kistemaker wrote that the promises themselves "are an important part of this verse, for Peter describes them as 'very great and precious.' Observe that he uses the superlative form to depict these promises. With the perfect tense *he has given*, he implies that God not only has given these promises to us but also has fulfilled them in the person and work of Christ."[104] This is another expressive portrait of the gospel's work. This is very different than the state of those who Peter saw as attacking the church in 2 Peter. According to Callan, Peter viewed believers as destined to receive the promises and avoid judgment, but he compared the false teachers to irrational animals (1:5), which the author intentionally used to maximize their shame.[105] The position of the believers was very different due to the

---

102 Harris, *NET Bible Notes*, loc. cit. "2 Peter 1:4."
103 Utley, *Gospel according to Peter*, 276.
104 Kistemaker, *Exposition of the Epistles of Peter*, 247.
105 Callan, "Comparison of Humans to Animals," 105.

divine power in 1:3 because of their supernatural calling through the gospel of the divine Christ. This is the background for 1:4, and the divine nature which Peter emphasized finds its meaning through that which was promised in 1:3.

The phrase γένησθε θείας κοινωνοὶ φύσεως (you may become partakers of divine nature) has been the source of much debate. Albert M. Wolters wrote, "This phrase has been taken, on the one hand, as explicit biblical support for the Greek Orthodox doctrine of θέωσις—the teaching that the goal of salvation in Christ is man's deification or divinization."[106] Christian Blumenthal described how a scribe attempted to lessen the divinity of Jesus in this passage in the Fayumic text because apparently he was not sure how to handle it theologically. The scribe even removed the very words concerning divine nature, seeking to change the entire christological orientation within the text. While retaining words such as Redeemer and Lord in a generic sense, the scribes had trouble with this idea. It appears they were afraid some would view the text as suggesting that humans could take divinity in essence and substance.[107] Others like John Calvin went so far as to entertain the idea of theosis cautiously. A. J. Ollerton observed:

> In his commentary on 2 Peter 1:4 [Calvin] concludes that the scriptural phrase 'partakers of the divine nature' refers to a kind of deification *(quasi deifican)*. This phrase shows Calvin's willingness to affirm the motif of deification (through explicit use of *theosis* terminology) whilst also using the qualifying term *(quasi)* to guard against certain versions of deification.[108]

As Stephen M. Clinton struggled with the clarity of this verse, he referred back to the verb γένησθε (you may become). He argued that the verb in essence communicates "so that you will become." It infers the work of the Holy Spirit to lead toward becoming a partaker of the divine. Clinton said that this is not a "direct participation in the divine, [that one has] become incorporated into God. Sharing in *koinonia* gives more of a sense of active participation—personal and intimate fellowship—which implies the same closeness and experience of divinity, but does not have the same metaphysical issues."[109] Schreiner, on the other hand, felt that the passage is rather clear, writing, "Sharing in the divine nature does not mean 'deified.' Instead

---

106 Wolters, "Partners of the Deity," 28.
107 Blumenthal, "Göttliche Natur," 280.
108 Ollerton, "Quasi Deificari," 237.
109 Clinton, "Theosis," 64.

Peter maintained that believers will share in the moral qualities of Christ."[110] Starr also left room for the possibility of Schreiner's view:

> The answer to that question is that it depends on what is meant by deification. If the term means equality with God or elevation to divine status or absorption into God's essence, the answer is no. If it means the participation in and enjoyment of specific divine attributes and qualities, in part now and fully at Christ's return, then the answer is—most certainly—yes.[111]

Who is correct? Does this verse describe a quasi-theosis as Calvin argued, an experience of divinity as purported by Clinton, or mere moral qualities as Schreiner held? First, theological difficulties and issues of scriptural unity concerning any idea resembling theosis certainly exist, whether quasi or otherwise. The patristics seem to have found clarity on this issue.[112] Brandon D. Crowe argued against such a suggestion, which would bring disclarity to the image of the Christian God, since such an understanding would find itself out of place in the context of the New Testament. He wrote:

> Peter is most emphatically *not* stating that we become God or a part of God. Fundamental to the biblical worldview is the Creator-creature distinction: the triune God alone is God, and no one or nothing else is God. This Creator-creature distinction will never change. God is perfect, without parts, and cannot be divided. Therefore, he cannot be added to. God is uncreated; we are created. Participating in the divine nature cannot mean that we become a part of God.[113]

Second, the divine experience of Clinton's view remains ambiguous, and one comes away with more questions than clarity. Third, the inconveniency of Schreiner's view is that Peter easily had the language to express to his readers that they would receive the moral qualities of Jesus. In fact, Peter used this language in 1:3, καλέσαντος ἡμᾶς ἰδίᾳ δόξῃ καὶ ἀρετῇ (called us by his own glory and virtue). Peter specifically used the words θείας φύσεως (divine nature), not moral qualities or ἀρετῇ (virtue). While Starr remained open for the validity of Schreiner's interpretation, ultimately he made a slightly different conclusion: "I propose that 'sharers in divine nature' should be read as theological shorthand for a constellation of ideas: knowledge of Christ producing escape from passion and decay to divine

---

110 Schreiner, *1, 2 Peter, Jude*, 295.
111 Starr, "Does 2 Peter Speak of Deification?," 90.
112 Ollerton, "Quasi Deificari," 237.
113 Crowe, *Message of the General Epistles*, 59.

moral excellence and divine immortality, both of which are in the process of being realized already now."[114] Ultimately, Starr's comment points toward the gospel as a deciding factor in 1:3, as that which changed the outcome for the readers. It is not merely different moral values that one receives to follow, as Schreiner suggested.

The passage suggests the imputation of the righteousness of Jesus, which Peter mentioned in the same opening thought, τοῖς ἰσότιμον ἡμῖν λαχοῦσιν πίστιν ἐν δικαιοσύνῃ τοῦ θεοῦ ἡμῶν καὶ σωτῆρος Ἰησοῦ Χριστοῦ (to the ones who received our same faith in the righteousness of our God and Savior, Jesus Christ). One has the ability to live a pious life (1:3) because the imputation of righteousness comes through justification. Peter did not use all of these specific words, but he described these theological ideas. The word κοινωνοὶ (partakers) has its root in the word κοίνος (common or companion). Because the believers received the righteousness of Christ through faith, they became companions of Christ. They shared in his righteousness. In 1:4 Peter described the believers as having tasted of Jesus' divine nature when he imparted new desires by means of his righteousness through faith. Due to the Spirit's work, who carries believers along, γένησθε (you may become), as companions of Jesus, believers receive a freedom to live in piety.

This all is only possible if Jesus is truly divine. Peter did not express confusion concerning the divinity of his hearers. Rather, he sought to clarify Jesus' divinity by way of attribution. Martin Williams underscored the companionship in which this takes place: "We experience salvation because the triune God, who is relational in his own nature, chooses to enter into relationship with us his creatures. He calls sinful humans to share in the divine fellowship (2 Pet. 1:4)."[115] Because Jesus was righteous, Peter declared that his readers may also be righteous through Jesus. This verse, in light of the context of 1:1–4, then does not merely encourage good moral living. Peter affirmed the gospel, by grace, through faith, not by works. The apostle Peter understood this gospel as well as anyone, according to his time with Jesus, the events of Acts 15, and his debates with Paul, which Paul referenced in Galatians. Peter even affirmed Paul's conclusions about the gospel in this epistle. In light of the context, the verse becomes clear. The phrase γένησθε θείας κοινωνοὶ φύσεως (you may become partakers of divine nature) represents the fruit of the gospel, not merit that one must achieve in order to earn God's favor. This represents a direct attribution of Jesus' divinity.

Believers are able only to taste what the divine nature is through the imputed righteousness, that is, the promises (ἐπαγγέλματα) of the gospel,

---

114 Starr, "Does 2 Peter Speak of Deification?," 84.
115 Williams, *Doctrine of Salvation*, 229.

καλέσαντος ἡμᾶς ἰδίᾳ δόξῃ καὶ ἀρετῇ (called us by his own glory and virtue), from Jesus, who is divine. One can no more have divine communion with one who is God-like than one can taste salt from a cracker sprinkled with something that is salt-like. In order to taste, share, commune, or partake in the divine, the divine must be present. Second Peter presents Jesus not as an imitation of God, but as God. Therefore, θείας κοινωνοὶ φύσεως (partakers of divine nature) speaks to the riches of Jesus' divinity by means of attribution.

A believer's nature surely changes through faith. However, according to Peter in 1:4, one does not become divine, but receives the fruit of the gospel or access to the ability to live a pious life in reaction to the working of the divine. Helyer agreed with this view and even held that the main problem with the false teachers was that they were "'shortsighted and blind' when it comes to 'the knowledge of our Lord Jesus Christ' (2 Pet 1:8–9). They fail to realize that it was Christ's 'divine power" that enables them to 'escape from the corruption that is in the world . . . and . . . become participants of the divine nature.' 2 Pet 1:3–4)."[116] Helyer noted that lack of knowledge, Peter's way of speaking of the gospel in 2 Peter, was the problem. The believers, on the other hand, had the gospel, and they were companions of the righteousness of Jesus, not on their own accord, but due to their knowledge or belief in the gospel. Peter affirmed that while the believers would never become divine themselves, they would become companions of the divine. That companionship would even shape their lives so that they would even begin to demonstrate qualities as fruit and therefore evidence of a living faith and imputed righteousness. By way of attribution, Peter clearly affirmed the deity of Jesus in the description of his divine nature.

INDIRECT REFERENCES TO JESUS' DIVINITY

Bauckham wrote, "What is clear is that Jesus is never mentioned in 2 Peter without a title. He is either named by his title ('the Lord') or else in the eight places where 'Jesus' appears a title is included."[117] While Peter filled the lines of his epistle with christological titles, it is also true that other indirect references to Jesus exist, specifically his deity. While not always with formal titles, Peter did describe Jesus dually in the affirmation of his deity. First, Peter likely referred to Jesus as Glory in three instances. The examination will assess Peter's usage of the term in 2:10, the clearest reference, and subsequently examine 1:3 and 1:17 in support of the argument. Second,

---

116 Helyer, *Life and Witness of Peter*, 219.
117 Davids, *Theology of James, Peter, and Jude*, 235.

Peter described Jesus as Master Redeemer. However, Peter formulated the description using his own style and unique vocabulary in 2:11.

Jesus as Glory

Second Peter is full of christological titles, especially those referencing the deity of Jesus. While other attributions and indirect references exist, the reference to Jesus as Glory is not hidden, but to the modern reader it does not present itself as immediately apparent. Horst Balz and Wolfgang Shrage noted that in the Petrine Epistles this is often the case with their Christology. It is wholly present, but Peter formulated it much differently than other New Testament writers, mainly Paul. This difference in style and description may be why Peter felt Paul was difficult to understand (3:16). They wrote, not many "christological confessions and songs [exist], which played a meaningful role. The few christological statements are not formulated explicitly, and they come across rather formal and docetic; what is emphasized is his divine lordship and amazing power, his transmission of revelation through his Apostles [recognized by believers]."[118] It is through this lens, Jesus' divine lordship, that Peter presented Jesus as Glory. The theme of Jesus as Glory is one that is also present as a major theme of 1 Peter. Charles H. Talbert wrote:

> The author could have stressed the theme of resurrection, as does Paul in 1 Corinthians 15, to establish a foundation for Christian hope, but he, unlike Paul, is not interested in discussing the resurrection but in developing the theme of glory (*doxa*). A review of the texts where this term appears in 1 Peter shows that it refers to the glory that God has given Jesus.[119]

Concerning 2 Peter and its broad context, Watson and Callan remarked, ". . . it is most likely that the glories are God and Jesus, since they are the ones said in 2 Peter to have glory."[120] Therefore, the theme of Jesus as Glory is part of the Petrine narrative and key to understanding his Christology, here specifically concerning Jesus' divinity.

---

[118] Author's translation; Balz and Shrage, *Katholischen Briefe*, 123.
[119] Talbert, *Perspectives*, 133.
[120] Watson and Callan, *First and Second Peter*, 190.

Exegetical Exposition of 2 Peter 2:10; 1:3, 17

2 Peter 2:10: μάλιστα δὲ τοὺς ὀπίσω σαρκὸς ἐν ἐπιθυμίᾳ μιασμοῦ πορευομένους καὶ κυριότητος καταφρονοῦντας. τολμηταὶ αὐθάδεις, δόξας οὐ τρέμουσιν βλασφημοῦντες.

But especially those who follow after flesh in its defiled desire and despise authority. Daring, self-pleasing, they do not tremble as they blaspheme the Glorious Ones.

Confusion exists concerning the identification of δόξας (Glorious Ones). Schreiner, Kistemaker, and Bauckham all held views that either identify δόξας (Glorious Ones) with angelic beings, as did the translators of the New American Standard Version, or as the apostles or authority within the church. Bauckham wrote confidently:

> The possibility that δόξας refers to human authorities, ecclesiastical (Bigg, Green) or civil (Luther, Calvin, Reicke), can be ruled out at once, for it can make not good sense of v 11. We must take δόξας, as in Jude 8, to refer to angelic powers. In that case there are two possible interpretations. Either (a) δόξας are evil angels and κατ'αὐτῶν refers to these δόξας (so most commentators); or (b) δόξας are good angels, identical with the ἄγγελοι, and κατ'αὐτῶν refers to the false teachers.[121]

Callan, however, held a different view, arguing that the aforementioned commentators made the mistake of viewing 2 Peter too much in light of the book of Jude. He wrote:

> In 2 Peter 2:10, using language borrowed from the letter of Jude, the author criticizes the false teachers for slandering the δόξας. This is usually understood to refer to church or secular leaders, to angels, either good or evil. These interrelations may be too much influenced by Jude's use of the word. In the context of 2 Peter it is most likely that the δόξας are God and Jesus, since they are the ones said in 2 Peter to have glory—God in 1:1; Jesus in 1:3; and 3:18. The false teachers' slander of God and Jesus is their skepticism about Jesus' return and all that will accompany it.[122]

Callan's view is preferable for a number of reasons. First, Peter described those who have fallen prey and defiled themselves due to their flesh's desire as having defiled authority, κυριότητος καταφρονοῦντας. It would then

---

121 Bauckham, *Jude, 2 Peter*, 261.
122 Callan, "Christology of Second Peter," 255.

be unexplainable and quite strange in the very next statement to build a similar statement in other words to refer to the church's human authorities and teachers. Second, it is highly unlikely that a Jew would use a form of the word δόξας (Glorious Ones) to describe a mere human. Surely, Peter was not attributing divinity to the apostles or church authority. While Christianity presented an alternate interpretation of the Hebrew Scriptures than what the religious teachers presented in this time period, it is illogical to imagine that Peter would describe a type of theosis. Third, as Callan noted, Peter described the divine Jesus and distinctly God as having glory in other passages in the epistle.[123] Fourth, 2 Peter's mention of angels in 2:11 makes best sense in the context when δόξας (Glorious Ones) describes God and Jesus. Peter argued in 2:11 that even the most powerful angels would not dare blaspheme the Lord in the way the false teachers did. If Peter wanted to speak of the blasphemy of angels and not the Lord, what theological point did he make? Did Peter encourage the false teachers to fear blaspheming angels? The meaning is immediately unclear, and it goes against basic hermeneutical rules of understanding a text, since a clearer meaning exists.

Callan's interpretation provided clarity to the passage without difficulty. If Peter referred to δόξας (Glorious Ones) as God and Jesus, then 2:10 speaks to an intensification of authority within the church. Therefore, God can save even those (2:9) who have fallen prey to the flesh and despised their earthly ecclesiastical authorities, κυριότητος καταφρονοῦντας. However, they did not tremble, τρέμουσιν, before God and Jesus, δόξας, as the author implied that they should. Rather, they dared, τολμηταί, Jesus with the outworking of their own blasphemous selfish desires, αὐθάδεις. Second Peter's description in 2:10 of Jesus as Glory again references the glory that God does not share. The plural noun δόξας (Glorious Ones) implies the aspect of the triune God. If God cannot and will not share his glory, Peter likely made reference indirectly to Jesus' deity when he used Glory as a plural noun to describe Jesus where he is also mentioned.

> 2 Peter 1:3: Ὡς πάντα ἡμῖν τῆς θείας δυνάμεως αὐτοῦ τὰ πρὸς ζωὴν καὶ εὐσέβειαν δεδωρημένης διὰ τῆς ἐπιγνώσεως τοῦ καλέσαντος ἡμᾶς ἰδίᾳ δόξῃ καὶ ἀρετῇ.
>
> Because his divine power has granted us everything necessary for life and piety through the full knowledge of him who called us by his own glory and virtue.

As argued in a previous section, θείας δυνάμεως αὐτοῦ (his divine power) clearly refers to Jesus. Three times in 1:3, Peter referenced directly, and

---

123 Callan, "Christology of Second Peter," 255.

indirectly by inference, the third-person singular masculine pronoun, θείας δυνάμεως αὐτοῦ (his divine power), διὰ τῆς ἐπιγνώσεως τοῦ (through the full knowledge of him), καλέσαντος ἡμᾶς ἰδίᾳ δόξῃ καὶ ἀρετῇ (who called us by his own glory and virtue), of which all refer to Jesus. The δόξῃ (glory) and ἀρετῇ (virtue) describe Jesus. Concerning the combination of δόξῃ (glory) and ἀρετῇ (virtue), Bauckham wrote, ". . . ἀρετή is virtually synonymous with δόξα, and denotes the manifestation of divine power. The phrase is a rhetorical variation on θεία δύναμις and . . . refers to the incarnate life, ministry and resurrection of Christ as a manifestation of divine power by means of which he called men and women to be Christians."[124] The function of καί (and), especially in 2 Peter, as already cited, acts to emphasize the object receiving the description. In this instance, the difference between δόξῃ (glory) and ἀρετῇ (virtue) is not what Peter emphasized. Rather, he emphasized the sum of their total. He used them in a multiplying way to express practically synonymous words to speak of how glorious Jesus is, even though the author was certainly aware that each word actually had a slightly different definition, and he would apply them separately in different situations. So that the readers do not mistake Peter as using the term δόξῃ (glory) poetically, he used the term emphatically to indicate that the divine glory that made the gospel, here ἐπιγνῶσις, and their calling thereto possible. Peter indirectly, yet emphatically, declared Jesus as Glory in 1:3 to present him as divine to his readers.

> 2 Peter 1:17: λαβὼν γὰρ παρὰ θεοῦ πατρὸς τιμὴν καὶ δόξαν φωνῆς ἐνεχθείσης αὐτῷ τοιᾶσδε ὑπὸ τῆς μεγαλοπρεποῦς δόξης· ὁ υἱός μου ὁ ἀγαπητός μου οὗτός ἐστιν εἰς ὃν ἐγὼ εὐδόκησα.
>
> For when he received honor and glory from God the Father, and such a voice was carried to him, by the Majestic Glory: "This is My beloved Son, in whom I am well pleased."

Terrence V. Smith viewed this section as having a set of parallels to the ministry and life of Jesus. He followed one logical line of thought concerning the possible background behind Peter's inference of glory to Jesus: "2 Peter 1:16–18 reads like a version of the resurrection appearances, with its description of 'glory' coming upon Jesus on a mountain."[125] While Peter may have had this in mind during composition, one must not make this stretch in order to find an inference of glory to Jesus in this section. It is clear even without such speculation as to the background. A clearer parallel is not to the Gospels but to 1 Peter, lending weight to the unity of the

---

124 Bauckham, *Jude, 2 Peter*, 179.
125 Smith, *Petrine Controversies*, 82.

Petrine Epistles. Charles H. Talbert wrote, "'God . . . has given him glory' (1 Pet. 1:21). This particular element, whether expressed as enthronement or related to the theme of 'glory' is very prominent in [1 Peter]. The former forms part of the Christological schema employed and the latter expresses the relationship of the author's Christology to . . . his thought."[126] The idea of God giving his own glory to Jesus, who is also divine, here by inference, is not an idea found by a singular author. Rather, the evidence of 1 Peter, which references this theme at least fourteen times according to Talbert, shows that it was an important christological idea, which remained important to Peter as he presented Jesus as divine to his readers.

In 1:17, τῆς μεγαλοπρεποῦς δόξης (the Majestic Glory) clearly refers to God the Father. However, in light of 1:3 and 2:10, Peter made his inference concerning Jesus as Glory subtle, yet clear. Watson and Callan wrote, "And the glory that Jesus received from God is so characteristic of God that God can simply be called the Majestic Glory in verse 17."[127] Peter mentioned the transfiguration here. This was not an event of which he spoke philosophically, but an event at which he claimed to have been present. This bolsters the claim of Jesus' glory. Peter's readers likely would have known the story in the Gospel account, which described him as present for this event. F. Lapham held that Peter, "recounts the story at least as much to legitimize his own prophetic authority as the chief witness of this sacred event, and as a proof of the reality of the life to come—and thus, by implication, of the coming judgment—as for its Christological significance."[128] John Sherwood disagreed with Lapham's assessment and commented that Peter "flings a verbal dart at his pre-Gnostic adversaries with his use of ἐπόπται. A New Testament hapax legomenon, ἐπόπται had become by New Testament times a technical term used in mystery sects to designate those initiated into a higher knowledge."[129] It is not immediately clear whether Gnostics or pre-Gnostics were in Peter's view. If this was the case, Sherwood continued, "he did so to reverse their snobbish use of the word by excluding the false teachers from his circle of true eyewitnesses. Peter, with John and James, had personally witnessed Christ revealed in glory on the mountain of Matthew 17:1–8."[130] Just as John described in 1 John, Peter also held that glory is something that one can recognize, view, and behold.[131] Peter insisted that he recognized this

---

126 Talbert, *Perspectives*, 133.
127 Watson and Callan, *First and Second Peter*, 184.
128 Lapham, *Peter*, 161.
129 Sherwood, "Only Sure Word," 57.
130 Sherwood, "Only Sure Word," 57.
131 Kistemaker, *Exposition of the Epistles*, 247.

being bestowed upon the divine Jesus and that he was an actual eyewitness. He reinforced his position as he made a gallant claim, namely that Jesus is God, and his glory is no different than τῆς μεγαλοπρεποῦς δόξης (the Majestic Glory) of God the Father.[132]

First, Peter stated, λαβὼν . . . παρὰ θεοῦ πατρὸς τιμὴν καὶ δόξαν, God the Father gave Jesus honor and glory. Here again the usage of καί (and) connects nouns in 2 Peter that have a similar usage in order to make an emphatic statement. The τιμὴν καὶ δόξαν (honor and glory) was divine honor and glory because its source was also divine and even majestic, ὑπὸ τῆς μεγαλοπρεποῦς δόξης (by the Majestic Glory). Second, Peter spoke to Jesus' divinity by speaking in terms of Father and Son. A God who is a Father and has a Son must also have a divine Son. Peter described the Son, Jesus in this case, very clearly as divine.

Jesus as Master Redeemer

Peter also indirectly referenced Jesus' deity in his usage of δεσπότης (Master). This serves as an indirect reference to Jesus' deity. The text does not specifically name Jesus in relation to δεσπότης (Master), but contextual witness exists that points the interpreter to understand δεσπότης (Master) as Jesus. Also, the context supports the probability that Peter used this in order to reference Jesus' deity. The words κύριος (Lord) and δεσπότης (Master) act as general synonyms with slightly different emphases. In three other instances in the New Testament, according to Vincent, authors used δεσπότης (Master) "in direct address to God."[133] In five out of the ten instances the New Testament uses the term, δεσπότης (Master) is applied to a human authority. Peter used the word κύριος (Lord) as a divine title for Jesus, which has its roots in the Septuagint's usage of the word. Therefore, the probable application of δεσπότης (Master) in 2 Peter 2:1 is to Jesus, who is also called κύριος (Lord), its synonym.

Exegetical Exposition of 2 Peter 2:1

> 2 Peter 2:1: Ἐγένοντο δὲ καὶ ψευδοπροφῆται ἐν τῷ λαῷ, ὡς καὶ ἐν ὑμῖν ἔσονται ψευδοδιδάσκαλοι, οἵτινες παρεισάξουσιν αἱρέσεις ἀπωλείας καὶ τὸν ἀγοράσαντα αὐτοὺς δεσπότην ἀρνούμενοι ἐπάγοντες ἑαυτοῖς ταχινὴν ἀπώλειαν.

132 Perkins, *Peter*, 123.
133 Vincent, *Word Studies*, s.v. "δεσπότης."

> But false prophets also came about among the people, just as among you also there will be false teachers who will secretly introduce destructive heresies, even denying the Master who purchased them, bringing themselves imminent destruction.

Peter's use of δεσπότης (Master), like much of the epistle's vocabulary, is very rare in the New Testament. Bauckham believed that δεσπότης (Master) "is borrowed from Jude, but 2 Peter adds a phrase . . . because he has bought them . . . at the cost of his death, it is implied—the only allusion to the cross in 2 Peter . . . [as the] image of redemption as the transferal of slaves to new ownership was fairly common in early Christianity."[134] While Bauckham underscored an important point concerning Peter's usage of the cross and redemption in this verse, he attributed 2 Peter to Jude, a common view. Holding this view implies that one holds to a late, non-Petrine composition and reliance upon either a common source document or, more likely, Jude, if one holds to the late composition date of Jude. The major difficulty with this view is Justin Martyr's allusion to this verse as he dialogued with Trypo. He specifically mentioned the ψευδοπροφῆται (false prophets), which existed as contemporaries with the Jewish prophets and the current ψευδοδιδάσκαλοι (false prophets) of his own time. He specifically mentioned that his Lord forewarned the believers against such teachers. Justin lived from approximately 115 to 165 AD.[135] Therefore, one can learn from Jude's contemporary usage of vocabulary. If Peter wrote 2 Peter, he may have used Jude as a source. If Peter used Jude as a source, Jude was written before 2 Peter. This view also fits well with 1:1, which claims Peter as author. The interpreter then should look at Jude's usage of certain terminology as a tutor for understanding difficult passages in 2 Peter.

Callan argued that Peter used δεσπότης (Master) as synonymous with κύριος (Lord). He argued that Jude refers to Jesus with both words. Jude 4 designates Jesus more clearly as δεσπότης (Master), probably because Jude sought to clarify that which he read in 2 Peter. Whereas Peter used ἀγοράσαντα αὐτοὺς δεσπότην (denying the Master), Jude made an explicit reference to Jesus and used the title κύριος (Lord) in the description's place. Callan concluded:

> This implies an understanding of how Jesus saves . . . by purchasing his followers from those to whom they are enslaved . . . . 2 Peter says nothing about how Jesus made this purchase. The language of purchase is also used in Revelation 14:4 without explanation of how the purchase was made, and in 1 Corinthians

---

134 Bauckham, *Jude, 2 Peter*, 240.
135 Kruger, "Authenticity of 2 Peter," 654.

6:20 and 7:23, where it is only said that a price was paid. Revelation 5:9 says that the purchase price was the blood of Jesus. This may be presumed wherever the language of purchase is used. If so, the author of 2 Peter regards Jesus' death as the price he paid to transfer his followers from their previous owner to his ownership.[136]

The word Peter used, δεσπότης (Lord), is the type of language used between a slave and an owner. A slave during the probable time of the letter's composition had the expectation to call their master by the descriptor δεσπότης (master). Davids wrote, "The point is that Jesus the Anointed One has purchased these people as his slaves, and [the false teachers] are failing to acknowledge his authority."[137] The passage probably means that the false teachers did not act as if they knew Christ. They did not demonstrate their devotion to Jesus. Jesus expects his δοῦλοι (slaves) to follow and obey him wholeheartedly in faith and practice. Peter described himself this way in 1:1, Συμεὼν Πέτρος δοῦλος καὶ ἀπόστολος Ἰησοῦ Χριστοῦ (Simon Peter, slave and apostle of Jesus Christ). Charles Bigg wrote concerning Peter's usage of δεσπότης (Master), "[It] is a word which elsewhere in the New Testament is used of Him only by Jude 4. The Lord bought them and they are bound to purity of life. But by impurity men practically reject their Lord's authority and deny His δύναμις."[138] It is highly likely that Peter meant to refer to Jesus and his divinity with δεσπότης (Master). The meaning of δεσπότης (Master) is a lord in a master-slave association when it refers to a human. A. D. Chang noted that "when it refers to God the Father, it seems to emphasize God's absolute sovereignty and ownership probably by virtue of His work in creation. When it is used of Christ, the context seems to show that Christ is the sole owner by virtue of His redemption ... [and He claims] the ownership of the whole human race by virtue of His redemption."[139] Peter set Jesus upon the same level as God the Father with the employment of δεσπότης (Master) in conjunction with his language concerning Jesus' grand purchase, which he implies Christ made on the cross.

No doubt exists that Jesus acted as a divine substitute and Lord of God's own kingdom. While Peter did not write κύριος (Lord) in 2:1, he used δεσπότης (Master), which carries a much stronger force with it. While κύριος (Lord) can also mean mister, sir, or husband, "δεσπότης always refers to a ruler, whether on the household level (and so it is used of God in Luke 2:29)

---

136 Callan, "Soteriology of Second Peter," 550.
137 Davids, *Theology of James, Peter, and Jude*, 218.
138 Bigg, *Critical and Exegetical Commentary*, 272.
139 Chang, "Second Peter 2:1," 554.

or on the national level," according to Davids.¹⁴⁰ Peter used the clearer of the two forms, and Jude used both words. Jude likely wanted to clarify the churches' understanding that the strong language Peter used also described the Lord God. "Jesus then, is seen primarily as the ruler of the household of God or kingdom of God (the two concepts are overlapping), as the one who is to be submitted to and obeyed."¹⁴¹ However, the text not only highlights the mightiness of Christ, but the words ἀγοράσαντα αὐτοὺς (bought them) function to show that because of his divine power, Christ also frees, redeems, or saves them.¹⁴² Thus, Peter described Jesus as Master Redeemer. The Master purchased them to redeem them. This was not a common practice at the time, but it surely reflected the attitude of early believers and slave owners who sought to follow this spiritual pattern in the physical world, buying slaves and freeing them.

Paul's letter to Philemon concerning the reconciliation of Onesimus is one example of the way the gospel challenged believers from different backgrounds as they navigated the meaning of authority and redemption. On the one hand, only God himself was worthy of the designation in this case to be called δεσπότης (Master) due to his great power and sovereign control. On the other hand, only God, as demonstrated through God the Son, Jesus, was so loving that he acted as a substitute on the cross to pay for sins that he did not commit, to save a people who did not deserve it. While indirect, due to these characteristics only God could fulfill this action through the Second Person of the Trinity, Jesus. This verse pointed readers clearly to Jesus and his divinity. Peter's use of this type of language should come as no surprise to his audience.

Paul W. Felix discussed similar terminology employed by 1 Peter to describe redemption, a purchase made through shed blood, in his discussion on penal substitution.¹⁴³ Kruger also mentioned this remarkable connection, writing, "ἀγοράσαντα in 2 Peter 2:1 speaks of whom Christ 'bought' with his blood and 1 Peter 1:18 speaks of how we have not been redeemed with perishable things, such as silver or gold, but with the imperishable, i.e. the blood of Christ."¹⁴⁴ This passage demonstrates a very clear picture of Jesus' work on the cross. Whereas in 1:9 Peter referenced "being του καθαρισμού των πάλαι αύτου αμαρτιών, which is very common language referring to Christ's atoning work," Peter connected the idea to those who

---

140 Davids, *Letters of 2 Peter and Jude*, 151.
141 Davids, *Letters of 2 Peter and Jude*, 151.
142 Bratcher, *Translator's Guide*, 146.
143 Felix, "Penal Substitution," 178.
144 Kruger, "Authenticity of 2 Peter," 659.

deny this writing τον ἀγοράσαντα αυτούς δεσπότην αρνούμενοι (denying the Master who bought them) in 2:1.[145] While the question arises of why Peter did not speak more of the cross in 2 Peter, Kruger answered that the interpreter must keep in mind the context of 2 Peter, which concerns the rebuttal and discipline of false teachers. He wrote, "[This was] a very different purpose than that of 1 Peter, and thus we should not expect the same emphasis. In the midst of 2 Peter's purpose the cross of Christ is presupposed and forms a backdrop for all his exhortations."[146]

As established by the demonstrative use of καί in 2:1, which finds itself between and indicative verb and a participle, bringing two ideas together, it acts as an adverb; καί acts here as the English idea of "even." The false teachers had denied the work of Christ, and by inference they likely unknowingly logically denied his divinity. This was indeed the heresy of the false teachers. At the same time, Peter's mention of their lack of correct recognition of the work of Christ on the cross also affirmed his own christological understanding of Jesus as divine.[147]

PETRINE CHRISTOLOGY OF DIVINITY IN THE NEW TESTAMENT

This chapter has examined the titles 2 Peter used to speak of Jesus' divinity and provided exegetical, expositional, textual, and circumstantial evidence. At the same time the author assessed various arguments against the deity of Christ, where they exist, and established the shortcomings of each. Peter demonstrated a consistent and high Christology in 2 Peter. First, Peter's christological content is consistent in that it fits well with the overall picture of his Christology elsewhere in the New Testament. Second, his particular expression of Christology is notable within the New Testament corpus.

Peter's Christology of Jesus' divinity is consistent with that which one finds in other Petrine passages in the New Testament. For instance, in A. Dennis Koger Jr.'s dissertation on the theology of Peter in the New Testament, he noted that in Peter's speech at the opening of Acts at Pentecost, he expressed an early and high Christology when he designated Jesus as παῖς (Son) in reference to his divinity, God the Son, reasoning that a son of a deity must also be divine, while Peter presented Jesus' divinity in 2 Peter in connection with his Sonship as well.[148] Peter's designation of Jesus as θεός

---

145 Kruger, "Authenticity of 2 Peter," 667.
146 Kruger, "Authenticity of 2 Peter," 667.
147 Titrud, "Function of καί," 246.
148 Koger, "Distinctive Petrine Theology," 215.

(God) is notable as it represents his high Christology and one of the clearest affirmations of Jesus' divinity in the New Testament. John 1:1, 20:28, and Hebrews 1:8 are the only other passages that speak of Jesus' divinity in such clear terms.[149]

Of all these instances, 2 Peter's title it gives Jesus represents the pinnacle of an author's affirmation of Christ's divinity. While the rest of the New Testament surely affirms Christ's deity, the aforementioned passages are by far the clearest to the reader. John 1:18, Romans 9:5, Titus 2:13, and 1 John 5:20 also affirm the deity of Christ, but interpreters generally classify their affirmations, descriptions, and titles in a B-class compared to that of 2 Peter 1:1. The only other place in the entire New Testament where an author uses θείας is in Acts 17:29. In this instance Luke used the word to refer to God himself. While only John and Hebrews may represent a higher Christology in terms of their development, according to Watson and Callan, "by calling Jesus by the title 'God,' the author of 2 Peter presents one of the most exalted evaluations of Jesus to be found in the New Testament."[150]

When one compares Peter's Christology in general, and specifically concerning the divinity of Jesus, with the theology of the other General Epistles other than 1 Peter, one notices a clear distinction. For instance, in the work by Bruce Chilton and Craig Evans, they noted the following concerning 2 Peter when compared to James and the Pauline Corpus:

> James' Christology is far less developed than that in 2 Peter. While in James Jesus is 'our glorious Lord' (2:1) with an 'excellent name' (2:7) and probably 'the Judge' who is 'at the door' (5:9), James does not go as far as 2 Peter. In 2 Peter we read of the knowledge of 'Jesus, our God and Lord' (1:2), an ascription that is paralleled even in Pauline literature only in 2 Thessalonians 1:12 and Titus 2:13 (cf. Rom 9:5), although fitting with the type of statement found in John 1:1, 20:28; Hebrews 1:8–9. Less unusual, but still explicit is the reference to 'the kingdom of our Lord and Savior Jesus Christ' in 2 Peter 1:11 ('Lord and Savior' being a favorite title, cf. 2:18; 3:2; 3:18). However one interprets these passages, 2 Peter's Christology is far more explicit than that of James.[151]

Therefore, compared to most instances in the New Testament, 2 Peter is not only clearer in its statements of Jesus' divinity, but Peter employed the language of Jesus' divinity more often.

---

149 Watson, and Callan, *First and Second Peter*, 162.
150 Watson, and Callan, *First and Second Peter*, 162.
151 Chilton and Evans, *Missions of Peter*, 47.

Jesus' Divinity in 2 Peter   61

Peter's use of titles and his descriptions of Jesus' divinity present his Christology as emphasizing divine sovereignty. Davids argued that κύριος (Lord), χριστός (Christ), σωτήρ (Savior), and δεσπότης (Master) communicated very clearly to the audience of the ancient world. What the ancient world understood is that when they heard something, they should obey it.[152] Therefore, one gleans from Peter's Christology of Jesus' divinity his emphasis on following Jesus and his commands. For, this pattern and simple understanding finds its reflection in the narrative of the Gospels, when Jesus called him to follow and be a fisher of men: "Passing alongside the Sea of Galilee, he saw Simon and Andrew the brother of Simon casting a net into the sea, for they were fishermen. And Jesus said to them, 'Follow me, and I will make you become fishers of men.' And immediately they left their nets and followed him" (Mark 1:16–18, ESV). One sees this pattern in Peter's own life and here in his teaching.

In a way, Peter viewed Jesus as Commander, and Peter viewed himself as a type of soldier. Whatever the Commander ordered, Peter was ready to follow, and he expected those in the churches to follow Jesus in this way as well. Davids described Peter's view of Jesus as an "imperial ruler."[153] Each time Peter alluded to or spoke of Jesus, he used a title, κύριος (Lord), χριστός (Christ), σωτήρ (Savior), or δεσπότης (Master), which supports Davids' description: "The picture is of someone who deserves submission because he has delivered people and defeated their enemies. Jesus has given a 'commandment' and has a kingdom, a rule present now, but a rule that will be universal in the coming new age."[154]

While 1 Peter focused on the sufferings of Christ, 2 Peter focused on the glory of Christ. Even in 1 Peter 1:11, 2:21, 4:1,13, and 5:1, the author mentioned the sufferings of Christ in light of a following glory of Christ.[155] Peter's Christology in the second epistle focused on the majestic reign and rule, but mostly assumed that the readers were acquainted with the gospel and the means by which Jesus saved those who believed in him. The author focused on Jesus' current work as the divine κύριος (Lord), who has finished his work and now rules as a loving authority, who bought and freed those who belong to him.[156]

Peter accomplished the task of presenting Jesus as fully divine in most instances by the frequency and specificity of the use of titles credited to

152 Davids, *Theology of James, Peter, and Jude*, 246.
153 Davids, *Theology of James, Peter, and Jude*, 247.
154 Davids, *Theology of James, Peter, and Jude*, 247.
155 Koger, "Distinctive Petrine Theology," 215.
156 Callan, "Soteriology of Second Peter," 550.

Jesus. Over time in the early church, most all of the titles κύριος (Lord), χριστός (Christ), σωτήρ (Savior), and δεσπότης (Master) began to take on a significant meaning for followers of Jesus, so that each of them eventually became alternate names of Jesus. In the Hellenistic world, a divine name had a special meaning. Hellenistic people even used divine names in magic. Therefore, while certainly not invoking magic, Peter used the name and titles of the divine Jesus in order to evoke the authority that comes with the name.[157] Interestingly, in Acts 3:6, Peter and John healed a lame man, and they invoked the ὄνομα (name) of Jesus. For Peter's Christology, Jesus' divinity was not linked to a blind authority without any relationship to his moral quality; rather, it was tied to Jesus' goodness, that which he demonstrated when he purchased his children on the cross. The divine name not only represented the Hebrew God as the Old Testament presented him, but Peter presented the God behind the divine name as Jesus, who did not leave the world in agony, despair, oppression, defeat, and under the curse of spiritual and physical death.

Peter presented Jesus as the absolute authority who loved his people enough to lay down his own life and buy his own children, redeeming them with his own life. Peter's Christology was not only a cognitive activity, but his faith in Jesus' divinity influenced his entire ministry both practically and theoretically. Therefore, it is fitting that in Acts 4:12 Luke records the following after Peter and John applied the ὄνομα (name) of Jesus to the lame man who received healing. Luke wrote, "And there is salvation in no one else, for there is no other name under heaven given by men, by which we must be saved" (ESV).

---

157 Busch, "Presence Deferred," 523.

3

Jesus' Uniqueness in 2 Peter

In 2 Peter, the author emphasized the uniqueness or distinctness of Jesus by assigning broad categories to God and Jesus. Primarily, Peter focused on the distinction between the fully divine Jesus, as evidenced in chapter 2 of this work, as a divine Son, which the author will examine in this chapter, and God, who, while one with the Son, possesses certain attributes that the Son does not. Several scholars have noted the christological uniqueness of the way Peter wrote about Jesus and God. Peter H. Davids wrote, "So in 2 Peter God is still God and is referred to when discussing events such as creation or the deluge, events discussed in the Hebrew Scriptures, . . . but Jesus is God's appointed ruler; he is the Lord who is biding his time, waiting as long as he feels appropriate for as many as possible to be rescued."[1] Duane F. Watson and Terrance Callan noted, "Peter can refer to Jesus as God in one breath and distinguish God from Jesus in the next. This may be a calculated effort to maintain both ideas, though without explaining how both can be true. Though distinct from God, Jesus is so completely identified with God that he alone can be mentioned instead of God and Jesus."[2] Mark Allan Powell and David R. Bauer simply commented, "Though verse 1 appears to call Jesus God, verse 2 distinguishes Jesus from the Father in referring to the world of salvation."[3] The uniqueness of Jesus, yet his oneness with the Father, has caused a mixture of awe, bewilderment, wonder, and confusion for such

---

1 Davids, *Theology of James, Peter, and Jude*, 236.
2 Watson and Callan, *First and Second Peter*, 161.
3 Powell and Bauer, *Essays on Christology*, 159.

scholars. Everett Falconer Harrison wrote, "The author is in position to press the truth of God upon his readers because of his presence at the transfiguration, where the Father approved his Son. This event served to make more sure the realization of the promise of Christ's return and the whole gamut of prophetic revelation that owes its origin to the Holy Spirit (1:12–21)."[4] Harrison's perspective is preferable. He realized that what has been viewed with confusion, the distinctness of Christ from the Father while remaining one with the Father in his divinity, was a deliberate Petrine christological construction. Peter's description of Jesus' distinctness from the Father and the Father's distinctness from Jesus expressed an early Christology and one of the earliest expressions of that which contributed to a clear understanding of the Trinity, a bedrock doctrine of the entire Christian faith.

While the author of 2 Peter described Jesus in terms of his divine Sonship, he described the Father as Preeminent Author, Magistrate, and Deliverer in order to present God the Father and God the Son as distinct, yet both fully divine. Therefore, Peter presented Jesus as not only fully divine, but as distinct from the Father. This chapter examines the language in each of these specific categories and the manner in which it exhibits Peter's christological emphasis.

JESUS' DIVINE SONSHIP

Peter specifically presented Jesus in terms of his divine Sonship. This continues 1 Peter's narrative that God is a Father and Jesus is his Son. Davids underscored Peter's usage in 1 Peter and its differentiation to 2 Peter, writing, "God is primarily 'the Father' of 'our Lord Jesus Christ' (1 Pet. 1:3). While only 1 Peter says this explicitly, the title 'Father' is used in 2 Pet 1:17 and Jude 1 as part of differentiating 'the Father' from Jesus Christ."[5] Peter assumed that his readers understood the Father-Son relationship between Jesus and God.

Particularly, Jesus' Sonship underscores his divinity. A divine Being can only have a divine Son. Jesus, who receives all the highest praise and honor in 2 Peter from the titles associated with his divinity, simultaneously holds the honor of being a divine Son. Not only did Peter's Christology depend on whether Jesus is divine, but his entire understanding of Jesus rested on his understanding of Sonship as well. Second Peter goes to great lengths to denote this Sonship of Jesus specifically, even in its grammatical constructions, divine attributions, assertions, and by means of its descriptive language.[6]

---

4 Harrison, *Introduction*, 415.
5 Davids, *Theology of James, Peter, and Jude*, 24.
6 Bauckham, *Jude, 2 Peter*, 168.

Jesus as God's Son

The distinct title Peter gave Jesus in his epistle is ὁ υἱός μου (my Son). Peter used this title in apposition to the Fatherhood of God, θεοῦ πατρὸς. This is the only instance in the epistle where the words πατρὸς (Father) or υἱός (Son) occur specifically in reference to Jesus or God. The only other instance of υἱός (son) describes Balaam as the son of Beor in 2:15. Πατρὸς (Father) does not occur anywhere else in the epistle. Peter employed both υἱός (Son) and πατρὸς (Father) here expressly to enunciate the distinction of Jesus from God the Father, even though he called Jesus θεός (God) so clearly in 1:1.

The epistle's use of πατρὸς (Father) and υἱός (Son) does not point to someone unfamiliar with Second Temple Judaism; rather, in the context of the entire epistle, which quotes from the Septuagint, it underscores the author's knowledge of the Old Testament scriptures and traditions. In each instance where Peter quoted the Old Testament, he used the Septuagint as his text. Alfred Wikenhauser wrote, "Indeed the author is so familiar with [the Septuagint] that his vocabulary is saturated with it; of his 61 *hapax legomena*, 34 or 35 occur in the [Septuagint]. Only someone very familiar with the [Septuagint] could have written 2:1–10."[7] Peter demonstrated his knowledge of the Old Testament, and this lends weight to the acceptance of Peter as the author of the letter that bears his name. The context of the writer as he wrote this epistle is of a first-century Jew who not only understood his own background, but likely was forced to deal with Gentiles, who did not share his background. Peter likely also wanted to exhibit his leadership skills in the extremely multicultural world in which he lived.

Peter's understanding of the culture around him is also apparent in the letter. Daniel J. Harrington noted that Peter tried to demonstrate his savvy for his international audience and "develop a 'middle way' by showing off his familiarity with Greek language and ideas on the one hand and by insisting on Jewish-Christian eschatological consciousness and ethical seriousness on the other hand."[8] This prospectively places Peter in the time of composition in Rome or in another city where both Jewish and Gentile believers lived. Harrington also noted:

> While giving the impression of meeting the needs of Gentile Christians and inculturating the gospel, the author of 2 Peter clearly favors a somewhat traditional Jewish Christianity marked by respect for the Old Testament, lively expectation about the second coming of Jesus and a lifestyle that is appropriate to

---

7 Wikenhauser, *New Testament Introduction*, 503.
8 Harrington, *First Peter, Jude, and Second Peter*, 237.

Jesus' followers who expect to face their Lord and Savior at the Last judgment.[9]

Therefore, Peter's usage of πατρὸς (Father) or υἱός (Son) was deliberate and not the work of a second-century follower who was confused about the Jewish understanding and character of God. Peter demonstrated, as Watson and Callan wrote, that "God and Jesus are distinct; God gives Jesus honor and glory; God is Father, and Jesus is Son. However, they are closely related."[10] The following exegesis of 2 Peter 1:17 will examine this distinction in greater depth.

Exegetical Exposition of 2 Peter 1:17

> 2 Peter 1:17: λαβὼν γὰρ παρὰ θεοῦ πατρὸς τιμὴν καὶ δόξαν φωνῆς ἐνεχθείσης αὐτῷ τοιᾶσδε ὑπὸ τῆς μεγαλοπρεποῦς δόξης· ὁ υἱός μου ὁ ἀγαπητός μου οὗτός ἐστιν εἰς ὃν ἐγὼ εὐδόκησα.
>
> For when he received honor and glory from God the Father, and such a voice was carried to him, by the Majestic Glory: "This is My beloved Son, in whom I am well pleased."

The use of τιμὴν καὶ δόξαν (honor and glory) emphasizes both terms. The glory that came from God the Father was very glorious. The verse begins with λαβὼν (he received), which stresses the action of giving and receiving, which is important in the context. Peter stressed the great glory, which only comes from God as having come παρὰ θεοῦ πατρὸς (from God the Father). The use of θεός (God) and πατρός (Father) together is notable because it provides a qualifier for θεός (God). In 1:1, Peter clearly referred to Jesus as θεός (God). However, in 1:17 Peter made a major shift. His use of θεός (God) was no longer generic, but he employed it specifically in separation from the object of the one receiving the glory, ὁ υἱός μου ὁ ἀγαπητός μου (my beloved Son). Initially, ὁ υἱός μου ὁ ἀγαπητός μου (my beloved Son) brings to the mind of the modern reader the baptism of Jesus, when a voice came from heaven saying, ". . . σὺ εἶ ὁ υἱός μου ὁ ἀγαπητός, ἐν σοὶ εὐδόκησα (You are my beloved Son; with you I am well pleased)" (Mark 1:11, NA27). While the language is similar in 2 Peter 1:17 and Mark 1:11, Peter's reference does not appear to refer to this instance specifically, but rather to the transfiguration. For 1:18 gives the location of the instance as ". . . ἐν τῷ ἁγίῳ ὄρει (on the holy mountain)" (NA27). Since holy mountain, ἁγίῳ ὄρει, cannot refer to

---

9 Harrington, *First Peter, Jude, and Second Peter*, 237.
10 Watson and Callan, *First and Second Peter*, 184.

the plains of the Jordan River, the only other notable occurrence in Jesus' life that fits the context is the transfiguration. Therefore, the setting of 1:17 is the transfiguration. Robert G. Bratcher wrote that the statement means, "'God the Father honored and glorified him.' This may be stated, 'God the Father showed how great and wonderful Jesus is.' It may be as some commentators say, that the honor consisted in what God said about Jesus, and the glory was the light that shone there (see Luke 9:30–32)."[11] Therefore, the beloved Son of God the Father in this context refers to Jesus, who was with Moses, Elijah, Peter, James, and John on the Mount of Transfiguration. The voice that Peter heard on the Mount of Transfiguration was very similar to the voice that one heard at Jesus' baptism. Just as Jesus was distinct from the Father on the Mount of Transfiguration and equally divine simultaneously, so Peter presented him as equally divine yet unique in this passage.

Davids remarked, "This is the only time that [God] is called 'Father' in 2 Peter, versus three times each for 1 Peter and James. In this 2 Peter is similar to Jude, who only uses 'Father' for God in Jude 1."[12] Bauckham purported, "Probably God is called Father here because the sentence goes on to stress Jesus' sonship in the words of the heavenly voice."[13] This is the main thrust of Peter's narration. Jesus received honor and glory, which God the Father himself authorized. Upon this authority, God the Father said to God the Son, ὁ υἱός μου ὁ ἀγαπητός μου οὗτός ἐστιν εἰς ὃν ἐγὼ εὐδόκησα (This is my beloved Son, in whom I am well pleased).

Davids noted that this designation was "a formal designation of Jesus as world ruler. The author is careful to make a separation between himself and God in that the voice was 'borne to Jesus' from 'the majestic glory,' and that it was this voice that they heard, rather than saying that they had experienced it from God directly."[14] The author in no way lessened the weight of the divinity of Jesus by invoking his divine Sonship. Rather, he used the title of a world ruler in order to maintain that Jesus had all the authority and equality with God, yet he was distinct from God the Father.

In Jesus' distinctness from the Father, he was also the unique Son of God, not just a special son of God. Larry Helyer commented:

> Peter's understanding of Jesus' Sonship far transcends the metaphorical, adoptive sonship of ancient Israelite kings in relation to Yahweh (cf. 2 Sam. 7:14; Ps. 2:7). That he revered Jesus as the Messiah is clear, but more profoundly, he also believed that Jesus

---

11 Bratcher, *Translator's Guide*, 142.
12 Davids, *Theology of James, Peter, and Jude*, 234.
13 Bauckham, *Jude, 2 Peter*, 217.
14 Davids, *Theology of James, Peter, and Jude*, 216.

is God's unique Son, who is coming again in glory just as he appeared years ago on the mount of transfiguration. The radiant glory that emanated from Jesus on that occasion dramatically declared his divine nature.[15]

The mention of the transfiguration served to undergird the notion that Jesus was the unique Son of God. While Moses and Elijah were present on the Mount of Transfiguration, the Majestic Glory from heaven did not call them sons of God. In fact, the glory from heaven made no mention of Moses, Elijah, Peter, James, or John. The voice specifically called out Jesus as ὁ υἱός μου ὁ ἀγαπητός μου, "my beloved Son," not "one of my beloved sons." Helyer added, "Jesus of Nazareth is far more than a Davidic Messiah or a prophet like John the Baptist, Elijah or Jeremiah; he is the unique Son of God, the 'Beloved.' His self-revelation through his beloved Son on the mount of transfiguration is not an apostolic invention; rather it reveals the 'prophetic message.'"[16]

The uniqueness of Jesus demonstrated Peter's desire to communicate to his readers the seriousness of the situation with the false teachers. According to David Helm concerning verses 16–21, this section serves as an exoneration of the apostles' teaching that "Jesus is God's Son and as such is not only our Savior but our King. For the apostles, Jesus has been given the nations as his inheritance. As God's Son, Jesus sits enthroned above all the world's rulers and religious ways. Peter concludes unabashedly that a true knowledge of God must include a belief in Jesus as his Son."[17] Peter tied a general belief in God the Father to a necessary belief in Jesus as the unique Son of God. In order to believe in God, one must follow Jesus. In order to follow Jesus, one must trust the words that he entrusted to his followers and the leaders of the church, namely, Peter in this instance. Therefore, the gospel, which 2 Peter describes as the knowledge of God, comes through an orthodox belief in Jesus as the unique Son of God.

Peter did not merely purport a christological emphasis of the uniqueness of God the Son, Jesus, because he sought to make an interesting theological point. Rather, for Peter, the gospel, the core message of the entire Christian faith, lived or died based upon one's understanding and acceptance of Jesus as the Son of God. Davids added:

> The presentation of Jesus as Son of God in an ontological sense expresses the idea that Jesus is God and yet distinct from God. He is God in the sense that he was revealed to be Son of God at

---

15 Helyer, *Life and Witness of Peter*, 219.
16 Helyer, *Life and Witness of Peter*, 222.
17 Helm, *First and Second Peter*, 179.

his transfiguration. He is distinct from God because he is the Son, not God [the Father] himself. The author of 2 Peter does not explicitly affirm this understanding of Jesus as Son of God. Later writers did explicitly affirm it (e.g. Tertullian). And this understanding became part of the doctrine of the Trinity.[18]

While Peter did not explicitly use the words "Jesus is the Son of God," he implied Jesus' divine Sonship in the strongest and clearest of terms, without issuing a direct statement. By way of his strong and clear implication, he completely denied a oneness theology that ignores any differences in the distinct attributes and qualities of the Son and the Father. He underscored the beauty of the Trinity, here emphasizing the First and Second Person of the Godhead. He did not deny that the Son and the Father are of one essence, but he unmistakably affirmed that Jesus is distinct from the Father and that he is the unique Son of God.

THE FATHER AS PREEMINENT AUTHOR

Peter further distinguished Jesus as the unique Son of God in his descriptions of God the Father. First, Peter portrayed God the Father as Preeminent Author. Peter emphasized the Father's work in and through all of creation, before it existed, since he has no beginning. He presented him as Sovereign Ruler over all the events that take place in the entire world, at least in a general way. He did not speak specifically as to the way that the Father rules all of creation, but rather that the Father knows and controls all of the times, epochs, and seasons. Within this grand theatrical-like portrayal of God and his creation, the Father is also the one who moves people specifically to complete certain divine tasks. Peter portrayed God the Father as Preeminent Author primarily in three ways, namely, by emphasizing the Father as Creator, Ruler of Time, and Mover of Men. Davids stated, "God the Father remains in the background in 2 Peter. What is unusual is that God the Father recedes into the background. He is clearly there, but only in the narratives from the Old Testament is his presence front and center."[19] While Davids' remark holds true, Peter nonetheless used his descriptions of the Father in ways to differentiate his role and person from Jesus in his role as the unique Son of God and his person. Nonetheless, one finds a clear picture of God the Father throughout 2 Peter, but in a way that distinguishes him from the Son and that does not compromise the divinity, uniqueness, or distinctness of Jesus.

---

18 Watson and Callan, *First and Second Peter*, 184.
19 Davids, *Letters of 2 Peter and Jude*, 150.

The Father as Creator

First, 2 Peter describes the Father as Creator. The Father is not just creative in his approaches and in the way he has designed certain features of the physical and invisible world, but he is specifically the Creator who existed before the beginning. Paul also presented Jesus, God the Son, in Colossians as having been fully present in creation when he stated, "For by him all things were created, in heaven and on earth, visible and invisible, whether thrones or dominions or rulers or authorities—all things were created through him and for him" (Col 1:16, ESV). However, in Colossians Paul specifically emphasized the equality and divinity of Jesus, not his distinct nature. The Father, however, as Peter noted, was fully present in a special way during creation, in apposition to Jesus, who was also present but, as the Image of God, the Firstborn of creation, εἰκὼν τοῦ θεοῦ τοῦ ἀοράτου, πρωτότοκος πάσης κτίσεως (Col 1:15, NA27). Peter's use of Father is consistent with his background as a Galilean Jew. A. Dennis Koger Jr. analyzed the Petrine speeches in Acts and in 1 Peter and found this theme to be consistent throughout Petrine thought. He wrote:

> The investigation leads to the conclusion that Peter's view of God as 'Creator' and his reference to God as 'Father' are credible as expressions of his theology. Generally speaking, the evidence suggests that Peter held a theocentric perspective in which God dominated his thought. His use of the designations 'God,' 'Lord,' and 'Creator' is a reflection of his Jewish heritage from the Old Testament. His identification of God as 'Father' is a reverberation of his association with and his instruction by Jesus.[20]

Peter's understanding of God the Father as Creator, then, according to Koger Jr., rightly can be thought of as a reflection of his Jewish roots and of his time he spent with Jesus. Therefore, the Petrine Christology of the uniqueness of Jesus is simultaneously a mirror into Peter's perspective on Jesus as one of his closest associates.

Exegetical Exposition of 2 Peter 3:5

> 2 Peter 3:5: Λανθάνει γὰρ αὐτοὺς τοῦτο θέλοντας ὅτι οὐρανοὶ ἦσαν ἔκπαλαι καὶ γῆ ἐξ ὕδατος καὶ δι' ὕδατος συνεστῶσα τῷ τοῦ θεοῦ λόγῳ.

---

20 Koger, "Distinctive Petrine Theology," 212.

> For they hid this intentionally, that by the word of God the heavens existed long ago, and the earth was formed out of water and by water.

William Barclay held that Peter's description of creation in 3:5 is extrabiblical, writing, "As so often in Second Peter and Jude the picture behind this comes not directly from the Old Testament but from the Book of Enoch. In Enoch 83:3–5 Enoch has a vision: 'I saw in a vision how the heaven collapsed and fell to the earth, and, where it fell to the earth, I saw how the earth was swallowed up in a great abyss.'"[21] Barclay's connection to Enoch certainly sounds like a stretch, even conceptually. Peter did not specifically mention a collapse. Moreover, the only similarity to 2 Peter's account and Enoch is the mention of earth and water. It seems that Peter used the two in broad terms to accentuate the role of water and earth in creation, but even in the Genesis mosaic account no problem exists with the presence of earth and water. Bratcher noted that ". . . by the word of God [means] 'by means of his word, God [the Father]' or 'God spoke (or, gave an order).' This refers to the account of creation in Genesis 1, where God created the world by his commands."[22] Therefore, Barclay's assertion that Peter accepted an extrabiblical view of creation is without merit. The focus of the passage is not simply on the material in creation, but the Author of creation. God the Father himself played a specific role in speaking creation into existence, τῷ τοῦ θεοῦ λόγῳ (by the word of God). Bauckham insisted that this was Peter's purpose. He wrote, "Our author is anxious to stress that the world existed only because God commanded that it should."[23] Peter described God the Father as the ". . . Creator of the world and in control of the cosmos, a cosmos that consists of heavens, the earth, and Tartarus," as Davids noted.[24]

Peter distinguished Jesus from the Father for a specific purpose, namely, to make clear God the Father's role in creation. The Father's role as opposed to the Son's role in creation played an important function in Peter's argument against the false teachers. The false teachers apparently denied the coming of Jesus, and they may have even denied the Day of the Lord (3:3–7). In 3:4, Peter required his readers to consider the nonsensical position that the false teachers held. He even stated that which the false teachers themselves purported: "Where is the promise of his coming? For ever since the fathers fell asleep, all things are continuing as they were from the beginning of creation" (2 Pet 3:4, ESV). Helyer reasoned, "Peter counters by

21 Barclay, *Letters of James and Peter*, 402.
22 Bratcher, *Translator's Guide*, 159.
23 Bauckham, *Jude, 2 Peter*, 298.
24 Davids, *Theology of James, Peter, and Jude*, 238.

forcing them to face a dilemma: How can you accept the doctrine of creation without also accepting the doctrine of eschatological consummation? Such inconsistency diminishes the power of God that brought all things into existence by the mere word of his mouth (2 Pet. 3:5)."[25] Peter's distinction of the Father and the Son played a special role in exposing the false teachers' logical fallacies.

It was by the Father's own word, τῷ τοῦ θεοῦ λόγῳ (by the word of God), that he created everything. Douglas Harnik wrote:

> Creation is brought into being by the power of the Word and Spirit of God. Creation is again and again judged and renewed by the Word and Spirit of God. *This is the real world*. If creation is finally to be fully liberated and made new by the Word and the Spirit, the divine parousia must consume everything that now holds creation and history in bondage to unrighteousness, death, and decay. The coming fiery purification and glorious transfiguration of creation are not two events in a sequence; they are the double effect of the final divine parousia of the Spirit and Word of God. It is for this that 'the present heavens and earth have been reserved (3:7).[26]

Peter tied the creation to the consummation, and in turn provided a warning in the same breath as he affirmed the all-powerful Creator God. This was a specific function in Peter's theology concerning the Father. Peter surely implied truths about what this meant for the Son and his own word. In this instance, however, Peter accentuated the Father's role in this act. If God created the entire world, he is also capable of ensuring the promise that was made by his Son.

Never did Peter diminish Jesus' divinity when showing Jesus as the unique and distinct Son of God. Rather, exposing false theology concerning the Father led to a healthier and more consistent Christology. Peter effectively used the authority of the Father as Creator to undergird the importance of trusting the divine Son and his promises about his coming. Mocking Jesus and his promises, and thereby his work of redemption, is akin to mocking the Father's work he accomplished in creation by his own word, τῷ τοῦ θεοῦ λόγῳ (by the word of God). Peter implied that there are serious consequences to those who do not respect the Son, by the sure word of God.

---

25 Helyer, *Life and Witness of Peter*, 225.
26 Harnik, *First and Second Peter*, 178.

The Father as Ruler of Time

Peter also presented the Father as Ruler of Time. The false teachers Peter faced apparently mocked God for his timing and questioned whether the Father really is sovereign over time. Peter distinguished the Father from the uniqueness and distinctness of the Son by focusing on the physical qualities of the world rather than just the spiritual ones. Glenn W. Barker, William L. Lane, and J. Ramsey Michaels argued:

> A remarkable feature of Second Peter's world-historical outline is its lack of emphasis on the cross-resurrection event as the clearly delineated midpoint of the ages. This has led to grave indictments of Second Peter for suppressing the very core of the Christian message. Such criticisms miss the point of what the writer is doing. He divides history by means of outward physical events that change the course of nature rather than by invisible, purely spiritual realities such as redemption or the Holy Spirit. The reason for this is connected with the problem he faces. Christianity had brought about no tangible changes in 'the way things are.' It appeared that all things did indeed continue as they had always been.[27]

Peter's statement about how the Father views time gave a completely new perspective to his readers. The Father is not a human like the readers, and therefore he also does not experience or understand time merely in the limited way humans do, though he is perfectly capable of understanding how his creatures understand and process time. Peter presented the Father as having dominion over this time as a key distinguishing factor in comparison to his view of the Son, who has a different relationship to time, not because of ability, but because of cooperation with the will of the Father. In 2 Peter 3:8, one finds the most representative passage of Peter's understanding of the Father and the way he rules over what humans perceive as time.

Exegetical Exposition of 2 Peter 3:8

> 2 Peter 3:8: Ἓν δὲ τοῦτο μὴ λανθανέτω ὑμᾶς, ἀγαπητοί, ὅτι μία ἡμέρα παρὰ κυρίῳ ὡς χίλια ἔτη καὶ χίλια ἔτη ὡς ἡμέρα μία.
>
> But do not let this one fact be hidden from you, beloved, that one day for the Lord is as a thousand years and a thousand years as one day.

---

27 Barker, Lane, and Michaels, *New Testament Speaks*, 353.

Interestingly, Peter employed the word λανθανέτω (let this be hidden), which is in apposition to a form of the same word in 3:5, λανθάνει (hide). In 3:5, Peter said that the false teachers intentionally hid, λανθάνει, the fact about the Father and his role in creation and what it had to do with later destruction. In 3:8, Peter warned not to let this fact about the Lord and his time be hidden, λανθανέτω. The false teachers forgot something that had the potential to bring destruction upon them, and Peter warned the believers that they should not forget that the way they view time is not the way the Father views time. This statement that Peter used in 3:8 ". . . derives from Psalm 90:4 (LXX 89:4)," according to Bauckham.[28] It was known by those who were familiar with the Septuagint. The reader could find the creation story, which Peter mentioned in 3:5, and the flood, which he mentioned in 3:6 in the Septuagint. This is why Peter claimed that the false teachers had hidden it intentionally and forgotten it deliberately, λανθανέτω . . . θέλοντας (deliberately overlook). Since the readers could also find Psalm 90:4 in the Septuagint, Peter reminded them to be careful not to hide it intentionally and forget it deliberately. Peter's use of ἀγαπητοί (beloved) specifically proves that he directed his message in 3:8 to those believers whom he wished to encourage in the truth and against the following of the false teachers.

Peter demonstrated the Father as Ruler of Time in the way he described time in 3:8. Bauckham argued:

> Peter's readers may continue to expect the Day of the Lord which will come unexpectedly like a thief, but lest they succumb to the skepticism of the scoffers they must also consider that the delay which seems so lengthy to us may not be so significant within that total perspective on the total course of history which God commands. Because he alone has such a perspective, God retains the date of the End in his own knowledge and power, and it cannot be anticipated by any human calculation.[29]

Peter used the statement in 3:8 and turned it around to demonstrate the lack of anticipation, as Bauckham wrote. The Father stands outside of time, and for him time, while not meaningless, has a completely different meaning that mere humans are not able to grasp. Balz, Horst, and Shrage also argued that the meaning of the two statements is not that time is merely meaningless. They suggested that Peter had no need to restate the verse from Psalm 90 if that was what he desired to say. Rather, they wrote, "Human concepts of time are unfit to grasp God's timetable. If earthly categories are inadequate, then the delay of Christ's Parousia is no longer a problem,

---

28 Bauckham, *Jude, 2 Peter*, 306.
29 Bauckham, *Jude, 2 Peter*, 310.

which of course at the same time abolishes the expectation of proximity. God alone ushers in the Day of His plan."[30] Therefore, Peter presented God the Father in apposition to God the Son as possessing the specific role to rule over and even outside of all time at his choosing. Watson and Callan simply noted that the distinction of the Father from the Son in 3:8 underscores the point that the relationship within the triune Godhead is complex. Even God, specifically the Father, perceives time differently than humans. Through Peter's restatement of Psalm 90, he reiterated the Father's trustworthiness in keeping his promises. In this instance, Peter told his readers that ". . . God is not slow to keep the promise of Jesus's return and all that will accompany it. This implies that God directs the course of the world's history."[31] Due to God the Father's specific position outside of the realm of time, he can work in, around, through, and outside time. In this way, Peter presented the Father as the Preeminent Author of History and specifically as the Ruler of Time.

The Father as Mover of Men

In Peter's presentation of the Father as Preeminent Author, he presented the Father as Mover of Men. The Father gave men messages throughout the Scriptures. These messages were from God the Father himself in heaven, and God the Holy Spirit played a specific role, as well, each time when God revealed his message to the individual authors of Scripture.

Jerome Neyrey held that the author of 2 Peter spoke of prophecy at a much later time after Peter's death in order to combat a second-century heresy.[32] His argument was that the author needed an authoritative response to heretics in his time. Thus, he chose the apostle Peter as his pseudonym. The author chose to frame his position as having come from God himself and not man (1:21) in order to strengthen his position. Bauckham argued that the author never meant to pass this work off as genuine but wrote it as a type of testament tribute to the apostle Peter, which he claimed was not from a position of dishonesty.[33]

Concerning Neyrey's stance on the late date of composition of 2 Peter, Robert E. Picirilli has provided convincing parallels and citations of 2 Peter

---

30 Author's translation; Balz and and Shrage, *Katholischen Briefe*, 149.
31 Watson and Callan, *First and Second Peter*, 212.
32 Neyrey, "Apologetic Use of the Transfiguration," 506.
33 Bauckham, "Pseudo-Apostolic Letters," 477.

in the patristics, with which scholars previously did not deal or had not discovered, supporting a much earlier date of composition.[34]

Peter presented God the Father distinctly as acting with God the Holy Spirit in this role to communicate divine messages of Scripture, whereas God the Son was not active in the same way in this task. While God the Holy Spirit acted upon men also in his own way, he inspired men by the will of God the Father. Concerning the immediate context, John Sherwood remarked, "In what amounts to an example of synthetic parallelism, Peter restates in v. 21 the essence of v. 20 with further details on inspiration's mechanics."[35]

Within this context, in some of the strongest of terms in the entire New Testament, 2 Peter 1:21 presents the Father's distinct role in conjunction with the Holy Spirit in the process of the inspiration and transmission of the Word of God. Joel Stephen Williams discussed at least four clarifications of what the Scriptures mean when speaking of the Word of God. The clarifications are especially important when interpreting Scriptures like 2 Peter 1:21. They help answer the questions of what the author meant by the Word of God, which God inspired. He listed:

> (1) The 'word of God' can mean a word which came from God, in contrast to a word that tells of God. (2) The 'word of God' can mean the content of what God had revealed. It became a synonym for the gospel which was preached by Christ and the apostles. (3) The 'word of God' can mean the Word incarnate, that is, the pre-existent Christ who became flesh. (4) Since the 'word of God' refers primarily to the divine message, and since that message is contained within the Scriptures, the phrase is applicable to the sacred writings.[36]

In verse 21, it seems that the author meant the Scriptures, including the message therein.

Exegetical Exposition of 2 Peter 1:21

2 Peter 1:21: οὐ γὰρ θελήματι ἀνθρώπου ἠνέχθη προφητεία ποτέ, ἀλλὰ ὑπὸ πνεύματος ἁγίου φερόμενοι ἐλάλησαν ἀπὸ θεοῦ ἄνθρωποι.

---

34 Picirilli, "Allusions to 2 Peter," 74.
35 Sherwood, "Only Sure Word," 72.
36 Williams, "Inerrancy, Inspiration, and Dictation," 166.

> For by the will of man, no prophecy was produced, ever, but by the Holy Spirit, as they were carried along, men spoke from God.

Peter wrote 1:21 in a series of emphatic clauses. The negative particle οὐ (no) begins the first clause with γὰρ (for) in the emphatic second position. Peter emphasized his point that the will of man did not produce prophecy. Prophecy, the inspiration of Scripture, or the moving of men did not originate with men, but with God. The opening statement ends with an emphatic ποτέ (ever). If any question remained with Peter's audience about whether or not an exception existed to the rule of inspiration of the Scriptures and prophecy, Peter made it abundantly clear that the answer was "no, not ever," οὐ . . . ποτέ. D. E. Hiebert underscored Peter's emphasis, writing, "'Ever' (ποτέ), placed emphatically at the end of the statement, means 'at some time or other in the past.' Joined with the negative (ου) at the beginning, the assertion is that at no time in the past was it true that biblical prophecy 'was made by an act of human will.'"[37] Peter emphasized that it has never been true that inspiration came from man, and it will never be true. Bauckham noted, "No prophecy in the Old Testament Scriptures originated from human initiative or imagination. The Holy Sprit of God inspired not only the prophets' dreams and visions, but also their interpretations of them, so that when they spoke the prophecies recorded in Scripture they were spokesmen for God himself."[38] Peter described the key and distinct role of God the Holy Spirit as inspiring humans with prophecy that came from God the Father. Second Peter does not hold that Jesus, the unique Son of God, exhibits this role in the inspiration of prophecy. For, Peter made the point that Jesus did not just speak of himself, but the triune Godhead spoke as one about the promises that concerned him, and towards which his followers looked, as Paul E. Jacobs argued.[39]

Peter emphatically began the next statement with ἀλλὰ ὑπὸ πνεύματος ἁγίου (but by the Holy Spirit) in apposition to γὰρ θελήματι ἀνθρώπου (for by the will of man). The false teachers received their understanding of the Scriptures by their own will, but the apostles received their interpretation and even inspiration for their writings from the Holy Spirit, who bore a message from God the Father on heaven's throne. Therefore, Peter expected the readers to heed the apostles' teaching, which they received from the Father by inspiration of the Holy Spirit, which testified of Jesus, the Son.

---

37 Hiebert, "Selected Studies," 165.
38 Bauckham, *Jude, 2 Peter*, 235.
39 Jacobs, "Study of 2 Peter 1:16–21," 28.

Kruger showed that the connection of prophecy and the Spirit is not unique to 2 Peter, but it appears in 1 Peter as well, and the readers likely made a connection with what Peter wrote in the first letter upon reading the current verse. M. J. Kruger wrote, "Both epistles are concerned with prophecy. 2 Peter 1:21 tells the reader that no προφητεία (prophecy) ever came about by the will of a man, but that the πνεύματος (spirit) carried the authors along. 1 Peter 1:10–11 speaks of how the προφήται (prophets) spoke by the πνεῦμα (spirit) of Christ."[40] Speculating on what Peter meant by prophecy or the inspiration of Scripture, Pheme Perkins wrote:

> [The author of 2 Peter] refers to 'your apostles' as part of the heritage of the community (3:2) that is on the same level as the prophets and saying of the Lord. 2 Peter 3:15–16 sets Paul and his letters on the same level as the Old Testament. Presumably, Paul forms part of the group referred to as 'your apostles' along with Peter.[41]

Peter used each clause to qualify the last clause, ἐλάλησαν ἀπὸ θεοῦ ἄνθρωποι (men spoke from God). Whereas the false teachers were also humans, ἄνθρωποι, and they also claimed to speak on behalf of God, ἐλάλησαν ἀπὸ θεοῦ (spoke from God), so too did the apostles. The difference, as Peter qualified, was that the apostles' message, which they spoke on behalf of God, actually originated from God the Father, and was carried along by the Holy Spirit, whereas the message from the false teachers originated by their own will, θελήματι ἀνθρώπου (by the will of man).

The Bible Knowledge Commentary recorded, "What they wrote was thus inspired by God (2 Tim. 3:16). 'Borne along' or 'carried along' translates the word *pheromenoi*. Luke used this word in referring to sailing vessel carried along by the wind (Acts 27:15,17). The Scriptures' human authors were controlled by the divine Author, the Holy Spirit."[42] Peter likely emphasized the divine origin or the prophecy that he and other writers had received in order not only to demonstrate the trust that the readers could exercise but also to show how much he himself trusted the Scriptures.

Gregory Boyd suggested that Peter's trust relationship to the Scriptures and his statement of their divine origin represented a direct connection to his time with Jesus, writing, "Throughout the Gospels, Jesus expressed an unqualified confidence that Scripture infallibly communicates the will of God. He consistently referred to it when deciding matters related to faith. This attitude of trust was adopted by Jesus' disciples . . . throughout

---

40 Kruger, "Authenticity of 2 Peter," 660.

41 Perkins, *Peter*, 122.

42 Walvoord and Zuck, *Bible Knowledge Commentary*, 869.

history."⁴³ One sees this trust and its continual revival in church history. Boyd also wrote that this trust has carried over into the current time as well among certain groups of professing Christians, writing, "... with the Protestant Reformers, evangelicals hold to the principle of *sola scriptura*, that 'Scripture alone' is the final authority on religious matters."⁴⁴ D. A. Carson, Douglas J. Moo, and Leon Morris noted that for some groups, namely Roman Catholics, 1:21 and the inspiration of Scripture led "to mean that it is the church that tells its members how to interpret the Bible (cf. 'no one can interpret any prophecy of Scripture by himself'). But the passage says nothing about the church; it speaks of what God has done by his Holy Spirit. The writer is affirming the divine origin of Old Testament Scripture."⁴⁵ The view Peter held concerning inspiration is also consistent with what one can learn about him and his view throughout the New Testament, as Paul A. Himes explained:

> Peter's theology of prophecy in Acts 2, designed to confront unbelievers and offer them hope, is further enhanced by Acts 3 and then applied to believers in 1 Peter. 2 Peter then utilizes prophecy as an apologetic against unbelievers while simultaneously presenting it as the basis for the proper conduct of believers. From Acts 2 through 2 Peter, the theology remains consistent.⁴⁶

Peter distinguished the Father from the Son from the Holy Spirit in 1:21 in order to indict strongly those who had filled his readers with falsehoods. In doing so, Peter affirmed the unity of God, while at the same time affirming the doctrine of the Trinity and the distinct and unique roles of each divine Person. The lack of mention of Jesus in this statement acts as a silent emphasis for the distinct nature of the uniqueness of Christ.⁴⁷

The Father and Holy Spirit's roles in the inspiration and transmission of prophecy and Scripture do not preclude human interaction. *The Bible Knowledge Commentary* records, "They were consciously involved in the process; they were neither taking dictation nor writing in a state of ecstasy."⁴⁸ However, as Hiebert noted, "By placing the participial clause, 'by the Holy Spirit being borne along,' before the finite verb, Peter lays emphasis on the Spirit as the impelling agent in the production of prophecy. The Spirit, not

43 Boyd, *Across the Spectrum*, 24.
44 Boyd, *Across the Spectrum*, 16.
45 Carson, Moo, and Morris, *Introduction*, 442.
46 Himes, "Peter and the Prophetic Word," 243.
47 Bratcher, *Translator's Guide*, 144.
48 Walvoord and Zuck, *Bible Knowledge Commentary*, 869.

human volition, is the originating power in prophecy."[49] While affirming the Father and Spirit's roles in the production of Scripture and the distinct role that the Son holds in apposition to the First and Third Persons of the Trinity, Boyd noted that the New Testament does not tell the reader everything about the communication of the Scriptures.

> Scripture ... does not resolve many of the questions we may have about this teaching—questions that a theory of inspiration would presumably be designed to answer. For example, nowhere do scriptural authors demonstrate any concern with the issue of how much control God exerted over the authors he used and how much of their limited, culturally bound perspectives he left intact.[50]

While the Scriptures are clear, but do not speak to every topic or in as much depth as one may wish, a general picture of inspiration concerning the Father and Spirit's roles emerge from its pages. Peter presented men in 1:21 as divine mouthpieces that received inspiration and produced Scripture. Peter held his apostolic authority over the false teachers. Rudolph Pesch wrote:

> Peter is qualified to be the guardian of the true faith, who has the authority to interpret Scripture and tradition. Peter is empowered to ward off the emerging theological errors in the church: the 'error of the God-despisers' (2 Pet. 3:17), who lead a false life, promise freedom, and are themselves slaves, spoiled by their desires.[51]

Interestingly, the doctrine of inspiration, as espoused by 2 Peter, precludes an editorial process. While form, redaction, source, and literary criticism all have within their principles helpful tools to understand the Scriptures, they all assume an editorial process. Some forms of criticism are certainly more helpful than others. An editorial process communicates that the author felt that the original contained mistakes. Therefore, they corrected the text. In turn, Peter's understanding of the distinct roles of the Father, Son, and Holy Spirit and how each one involved himself in the inspiration of Scripture defends against a traditional editorial process. When the authors wrote, according to Peter's distinct understanding of inspiration, they wrote Scripture directly after receiving the final inspiration without need of a formal editorial process. Hiebert argued, "[The authors] were not, strictly speaking, passive, for each prophet showed, in the style of language

---

49 Hiebert, "Selected Studies," 166.
50 Boyd, *Across the Spectrum*, 25.
51 Author's translation; Pesch, *Biblischen Grundlagen*, 54.

in which he uttered his prophecies, his own mental peculiarities.'"[52] While the Scriptures do not explicitly say this, Hiebert explained what Scripture demonstrates, as one clearly sees when reading the different authors with different styles who claim inspiration.

Jacobs argued that "... [φερόμενοι] carries here the same concept or picture which St. Paul uses in 2 Timothy 3:16: [θεόπνευστος]—God breathed."[53] Helm argued that the etymology for the English word ferry is φερόμενοι (as they were carried along) in 1:21 and that the translator is accurate to communicate the idea of the Father and Spirit's word as such. He wrote:

> Peter argues that all the writers of Scripture were ferried along by the Holy Spirit and arrived at the same destination. One has to imagine these writers as cars aboard a ferry. Each one got on the ferry—each one appeared to be doing his own thing—each one delivered his own distinctive word. But at the same time the owner of the ferry—in this case, God—made sure they all landed together at his port of call because he carried them to their destination on the ballast and strength of his Spirit.[54]

Ben Witherington did not insist on such an illustration as Helm, which required the English understanding of a ferry. Rather, he likened the word φερόμενοι to an illustration fitting for the first century AD. He wrote that φερόμενοι (as they were carried along) pictures "... wind moving something along or driving it in a certain direction, or ... figuratively of God's Spirit moving or motivating human beings (cf. Job 17:1 LXX)."[55] Thus, God stirred and guided Peter and other authors of the Scriptures so that what the authors wrote on paper would be the very words God intended to pass on to his followers. In Peter's description of the distinct nature of the Father and Spirit from the Son, Peter affirmed that the message he received was not made by his own will or cleverly concocted myths, but from direct prophecy from God the Father himself by way of the Holy Spirit.[56]

Peter did not present a confused Christology. He demonstrated a very clear understanding of the Trinity, due to his own inspiration, which allowed for a special understanding even at such an early possible date of composition. While there is only one God, and the Father, Son, and Holy Spirit are God, they are distinct. Peter presented Jesus as the Son of God, but not specifically as the Preeminent Author who is active in the moving

---

52 Hiebert, "Selected Studies," 167.
53 Jacobs, "Study of 2 Peter 1:16–21," 28.
54 Helm, *First and Second Peter*, 219.
55 Witherington, *Indelible Image*, 791.
56 Himes, "Peter and the Prophetic Word," 238.

of mankind, even one's very thoughts. Peter presented the Holy Spirit as the one who gives inspiration, but on behalf of the will of the Father, by logical inference, as other scholars also noted in this section.

THE FATHER AS MAGISTRATE

Second, Peter not only presented the Father distinctly as Preeminent Author, describing him as Creator, Ruler of Time, and Mover of Men, but he also presented the Father as Magistrate. Peter accomplished this distinction primarily in two ways. He described God the Father as a divine Condemner and as a divine Judge. Therefore, the Father not only fills the role within the Trinity in a specific way of judging right from wrong, justice from injustice, and good from evil, but he also ultimately executes the sentence as well. Therefore, Magistrate is a word that encompasses his legal standing and role in the law of the world, which he himself created.

The Father as Condemner

The broader context concerns God's judgment and begins in 2:4 with εἰ γὰρ ὁ θεὸς . . . οὐκ ἐφείσατο (for if God did not spare). The micro-context in which Peter described the Father as Condemner is 2:6–8, while the broader context encompasses 2:4–9. The contextual backdrop and opening of Peter's language of condemnation, in which Peter presented the Father as divine Condemner, begins specifically in 2:5, καὶ ἀρχαίου κόσμου οὐκ ἐφείσατο, ἀλλὰ . . . κατακλυσμὸν κόσμῳ ἀσεβῶν ἐπάξας (and if he did not spare the ancient world, but . . . when he brought a flood upon the world). The Father did not condemn the world due to a wickedness of his own or due to an unrighteousness upon his own part. Rather, the meaning of the word κόσμος (world) in the context of James, John, and 2 Peter "signifies the world as organized by human beings against God, referring to its influences and fallenness. Thus, the author of 2 Peter is talking not about the good material (natural) existence that God created but rather about the bad society that human beings have perpetuated in the world."[57]

The backdrop for the Father's role as Condemner in 2:6–8 is that wicked people willingly chose not to follow God, just as the false teachers willingly chose not to listen to the Word of God. Thus, Peter warned those who did not recognize the unique Son of God, with whom God said he was pleased upon at least two public occasions, once at Jesus' baptism and the

---

57 Witherington, *Indelible Image*, 724.

Jesus' Uniqueness in 2 Peter   83

other on the Mount of Transfiguration. The text warned them that if they did not also recognize Jesus as the unique Son of God, God the Father had condemnation in store for them, just as he had in the history of the Old Testament.

Exegetical Exposition of 2 Peter 2:6–8

> 2 Peter 2:6: καὶ πόλεις Σοδόμων καὶ Γομόρρας τεφρώσας καταστροφῇ κατέκρινεν, ὑπόδειγμα μελλόντων ἀσεβέσιν τεθεικώς.
>
> and if by reducing the cities of Sodom and Gomorrah to ashes, He condemned them to destruction, making them an example of what is going to happen to the impious.

This is the second of a series of conditional statements Peter used to answer 2:4, εἰ γὰρ ὁ θεὸς . . . οὐκ ἐφείσατο (for if God did not spare), which start in 2:5. The language of condemnation, however, concerning the role of God the Father begins in 2:6. In 2:6, Peter clearly portrayed the Father's role in the Old Testament in the destruction of Sodom and Gomorrah. The main clause in the verse is τεφρώσας καταστροφῇ κατέκρινεν (by reducing to ashes, he condemned them to destruction). The rest of the ideas surround one main idea. The verb κατέκρινεν (he condemned) names its end result, καταστροφῇ (destruction), where the English word catastrophe has its etymology, and uses it in conjunction with τεφρώσας (reducing to ashes), a verb that qualifies the level of destruction. Peter presented God the Father as one who brings decisive destruction when he acts.

For the readers who may have erred, Peter provided the gravest of warnings, telling them that the complete and utter destruction of Sodom and Gomorrah was the example, ὑπόδειγμα . . . τεθεικώς (making them an example), of the destruction that the Father also has in store from them. While Peter presented Jesus as Master Redeemer, he presented the Father here as the Condemner who brings sure and complete destruction to vessels not glorifying him.

One finds very similar material in Jude and 2 Peter. This passage also is represented in Jude 7. Different views exist as to the reason for the shared material. Bratcher gave an overview of these views:

> A given explanation of the relation between the two will be influenced in part by the conclusion as to the authorship and the date of each of the two Letters. The obvious similarity between the two—nearly all of Jude is to be found in 2 Peter—has received several explanations: (1) Both letters are dependent upon a

common source, either oral or written. (2) Jude is dependent upon 2 Peter; very few hold to this view. (3) 2 Peter is dependent on Jude; this is the view of the majority.[58]

A fourth view exists, which many evangelicals hold, as Schreiner described in his introduction and background of 2 Peter.[59] In essence, the pervasive view among theologically conservative evangelicals is that God is equally capable to transmit Scripture to different authors, in different places, and even in different times, which appear to share much of the same material. The logic behind Schreiner's view is that if an all-powerful God inspires Scripture, and if he indeed created the entire world by speaking it into being, it is certainly within his ability to inspire Scripture so as to bring about similarities and even exact representations of portions of Scripture through different authors for his own purposes and motivations.

Terrance Callan wrote the following comment assuming 2 Peter's dependence upon Jude. He commented directly on the thrust of the current passage.

> The author of 2 Peter changed the main verb of Jude 7 from "serve" to "condemned," making it clear that God was responsible for the destruction of Sodom and Gomorrah. 2 Peter changed the description of the destruction from "undergoing a punishment of eternal fire" to "having turned [them] to ashes." Perhaps the author thought this was a more accurate description of the fate of the two cities.[60]

Regardless of whether or not one holds that Peter relied on another document, Callan demonstrated that Peter clearly emphasized God's action in the condemnation and judgment of the cities. Peter described Jesus as κύριος (Lord), as the author of this work examined in the second chapter, and thereby incorporated the imagery of a deity who exercises complete ownership over his people. In contrast, he described the Father's role as the First Person of the Trinity as the one who executes discipline, punishment, wrath, and destruction.

Peter described the destruction of Sodom and Gomorrah to tell about one of God's examples to mankind and warn against impiety. This was certainly a familiar theme to Peter as a Jew, and it would have been a common understanding of the Old Testament deity for those of his readers acquainted with these narratives. Boyd wrote:

---

58 Bratcher, *Translator's Guide*, 2.
59 Schreiner, *1, 2 Peter, Jude*, 27.
60 Callan, "Use of Jude," 51.

The Old Testament has a good deal to say about the ultimate destiny of those who resist God. Peter specifically cites the destruction of Sodom and Gomorrah as a pattern how God judges the wicked. The Lord turned the inhabitants of these cities "to ashes" and "condemned them to extinction," thus making "them an example of what is coming to the ungodly" (2 Pet. 2:6). Conversely, the Lord's rescue of Lot sets a pattern for how the Lord will "rescue the godly from trial" (2 Pet. 2:9). There is thus a precedent in the New Testament for learning about the fate of the wicked in the Old Testament: The wicked are "condemned ... to extinction." Throughout the Old Testament, the Lord threatens the wicked with annihilation. To all who refuse to comply with the covenant God had established, for example, the Lord vows to "blot out their names from under heaven" (Deut. 29:20).[61]

Boyd argued that Peter cited the Old Testament and that his readers accepted it as history. Peter's readers did not separate their spiritual meaning from their historicity. He warned the readers of the complete condemnation that God the Father is capable of carrying out, just as he carried out in the written historical past.

2 Peter 2:7–8: καὶ δίκαιον Λὼτ καταπονούμενον ὑπὸ τῆς τῶν ἀθέσμων ἐν ἀσελγείᾳ ἀναστροφῆς ἐρρύσατο, βλέμματι γὰρ καὶ ἀκοῇ ὁ δίκαιος ἐγκατοικῶν ἐν αὐτοῖς ἡμέραν ἐξ ἡμέρας ψυχὴν δικαίαν ἀνόμοις ἔργοις ἐβασάνιζεν.

and if He rescued righteous Lot, worn down by the licentious behavior of the lawless, he saw and heard the righteous man, living among them, day by day his righteous soul tormented by their lawless deeds.

When first reading through 2:7–8, the connection to the Father as Condemner may not be so clear as one may desire. However, Bauckham argued that Peter carefully mentioned Lot and his moral dilemma in Sodom and Gomorrah as another strict warning to his readers, who may have also needed to reconsider their own moral compasses. Bauckham wrote, "The point of this extended description of Lot's righteous distress must be to heighten the contrast between the righteous whom God delivers and the wicked he punishes, and hopefully to echo the feelings of 2 Peter's readers in their own situation."[62] Peter's readers likely felt distressed in their situation. Possibly, they thought that the specific immorality, ἀσελγεία ἀναστροφῆς (licentious behavior), that Peter mentioned was an accusation of which they

---

61 Boyd, *Across the Spectrum*, 287.
62 Bauckham, *Jude, 2 Peter*, 253.

were not personally guilty, and toward which they felt superior. Peter likely used this word somewhat provocatively, seeking a response from the readers. Kruger noted, "Correspondence is seen between ἀσελγεία in 2 Peter 2:7 and ἀσελγείαις in 1 Peter 4:3. This word is found only nine times in the New Testament and occurs in the above two references and also 2 Peter 2:18. Thus, three out of the nine occurrences are found in the Petrine epistles."[63] Likely, the readers felt that because ἀσελγεία ἀναστροφῆς (licentious behavior) was not their personal struggle, the discussion was not important to them. However, Peter used the provocative word ἀσελγεία (licentious) to show that Lot also had a choice to make, even though he found deliverance from the twin cities that the Father condemned.

The readers may have felt that they were caught in the middle of an argument between the apostles, leaders of the church, and the false teachers, as is often the case in such conflicts. It is often easy for those in churches to attempt to take a middle ground for the sake of false unity, hoping for a release from uncomfortable feelings that are associated with conflict. Pertaining to the dissidents in the community, M. Desjardins wrote, "[t]heir destruction is guaranteed in 2 Peter 2:3, while in 2:12–13a the author compares them to 'animals born to be caught and killed'. A few verses later he states that they can expect a punishment even more severe than that reserved for non-Christians (2:20–21)."[64] Peter emphasized their condemnation, and he evoked the role of God the Father as Condemner in this situation to show that he not only dealt swiftly with the evil people in Sodom and Gomorrah, but he was ready to do the same with Lot had he chosen a different path and trusted those in his city rather than God, his Heavenly Father. In essence, Lot forced himself to make a decision to follow God that was in direct opposition to almost every resident in the entire region of the twin cities. This decision was surely difficult, as it was also for Peter's readers.

It may appear that because God is merciful, he always finds a way around condemnation. In his dealings with his own Son Jesus on the cross, he also displayed not only his mercy but also his justice via his wrath and condemnation. Clearly, the New Testament argues that there is a way around condemnation but only through faith in God the Son. God was always merciful and so he remains. Peter did not present a Father who became more merciful because the Son incarnated. Rather, he presented a Father who was and is completely comfortable exercising divine condemnation even to physical death and utter destruction.

---

63 Kruger, "Authenticity of 2 Peter," 659.
64 Desjardins, "Portrayal of Dissidents," 92.

The difference in the New Testament and in Peter's Christology is that God's condemnation acted upon the Son. For, those who believed the gospel also found deliverance, according to Peter. Peter presented those who do not have the ἐπίγνωσις (full knowledge) of God, Peter's description of the knowledge of the gospel and implied faith, as culpable for their actions and condemnable. According to Peter, God the Father did not change in his role as divine Condemner because he also saves other people by his grace through faith in his Son. As Creator and Preeminent Author, the Father also has the right to have ultimate dominion, rule, and reign over all of his created people, and things both seen and unseen. Peter warned his readers that just as Lot had to be sure concerning in whom he ultimately placed his trust and followed in piety, so too must New Testament believers. Otherwise, Peter promised the believers directly, and by inference, that they surely would come to know the Father as Condemner.

The Father as Judge

In 2 Peter's description of the Father as divine Magistrate, the epistle not only portrays him as divine Condemner but as divine Judge. The Father not only actively destroys that which is evil, but he does so based upon his discernment, judgment, and decree. The Father's role in judgment as distinguished from that of the Son is a common theme in Peter's epistles. Concerning 1 Peter, W. J. Dalton wrote, "... [I]n the section [1 Peter] 3:14—4:11 ... we find a similarity of ideas and structure which could have influenced 2 Peter."[65] He demonstrated clearly that 1 and 2 Peter not only have many parallels, but that specifically God's judgment plays a key role. This was a theme often missed by other commentators, as Dalton illustrated. Kruger also noted the theme of the Father's divine judgment as playing a significant role in both epistles as well as in showing the distinct roles of each Person of the Trinity. He noted that this is especially evident when viewing the roles of each Person within the context of Peter's eschatology. Kruger wrote, "The second coming of the Lord is an obvious theme in both epistles. 2 Peter 2:9 describes it as the 'day of judgment' where the world will be destroyed by fire (2 Pet. 3:7). The readers are urged by the author to look forward to this time (2 Pet. 3:12)."[66]

Richard Mayhue interpreted the Day of the Lord as two different days, while traditionally seen as one day, the day of the return of the Lord, including his judgment. He believed that, based upon the prepositional phrases ἐν

---

65 Dalton, "Interpretation of 1 Peter 3:19," 550.
66 Kruger, "Authenticity of 2 Peter," 659.

ἤ (and then) and δι ἥν (because of which) in 3:12, Peter wanted to describe different days, one in which Jesus returns from heaven the same way he ascended in Acts, and a day of destruction. Peter believed that the destruction would produce an eternal blessing, which Peter called "the day of eternity" in the doxology of 3:18.[67] Mayhue's view is speculative at best. Peter provided no contextual evidence to suggest Mayhue's view, nor does the Old Testament provide an alternate definition or suggest the Day of the Lord could somehow be different days. Mayhue overlooked the important distinction that Peter made. Thiede wrote, "The idea of a cosmic conflagration is well documented throughout the Old Testament, and we may assume that a passage from the Torah, such as Deuteronomy 32:22, would have been a particularly important precedent for the author of 2 Peter as we know him."[68] The idea that the world will someday be judged, which will result in its complete condemnation, is not foreign to the Old Testament. Davids wrote, "The day of judgment can be called the 'day of God' (3:12), not just the 'day of the Lord' or some similar term. That places God at the end of the age as he was the Creator at the beginning."[69] Mayhue failed to see 2 Peter as a part of its biblical historical context. The Father was present as Creator in a sovereign sense, and it is his right to judge that which/whom he has created. Peter placed the responsibility for following, obeying, and honoring the Son on the Father, represented by the apostles. Therefore, Peter's distinction of Jesus as the unique Son of God placed the Father close to Jesus, but with a certain observable distance in terms of roles. The relationship between following God, who is capable of judgment, and obeying the Son, Jesus, likely created the fear of God in readers, as Peter intended. Peter's understanding, as a Jew who made himself familiar with the Old Testament, fits the current context, and it lends weight to arguments that support traditional Petrine authorship. It is not only possible that Peter penned 2 Peter, but it is likely, according to Thiede, who wrote:

> We note that the cosmic conflagration of 2 Peter 3:7, 10–12 is firmly established in a scriptural context that makes a first-century date much more plausible than any date *after* the turn of the century; that both Caecilius in the writing of Minucius Felix and Celsus as quoted by Origen are likely to have known 2 Peter, and that the *Octavius* belongs to the period of Justin, prior to Irenaeus and his fight against the Gnostics. We also note that the cosmic conflagration was a matter of serious, not just popular or

---

67 Mayhue, "Day of the Lord," 258.
68 Thiede, "Pagan Reader of 2 Peter," 80.
69 Davids, *Theology of James, Peter, and Jude*, 234.

mythological concern in antiquity, something we are beginning to understand again at the end of the twentieth century.[70]

Peter's contribution is not only his affirmation of the Father's work of divine judgment, but also that he specifically described this as a task that the Father uniquely carries out.

Exegetical Exposition of 2 Peter 3:7, 12

2 Peter 3:7: οἱ δὲ νῦν οὐρανοὶ καὶ ἡ γῆ τῷ αὐτῷ λόγῳ τεθησαυρισμένοι εἰσὶν πυρὶ τηρούμενοι εἰς ἡμέραν κρίσεως καὶ ἀπωλείας τῶν ἀσεβῶν ἀνθρώπων.

but the present heavens and the earth, by the same word, are being reserved for fire, held for the Day of Judgment and destruction of impious men.

In 3:7, Peter described the Father's decree of judgment over the world, here ἡ γῆ τῷ αὐτῷ λόγῳ τεθησαυρισμένοι εἰσὶν πυρὶ (by the same word, are being reserved for fire), and specifically over those whom God considers τῶν ἀσεβῶν ἀνθρώπων (of impious men). Bauckham stated, "Our author's point is that since the world was created by God's word and has already been destroyed once by God's word, we can confidently expect the future judgment which has also been decreed by his word."[71] The words ἀσεβῶν ἀνθρώπων (impious men) describe the sin of those to whom Peter pointed as the theme of God's judgment.

Mayhue stood alone in his specific interpretation of the passage that the Day of Judgment, ἡμέραν κρίσεως, is merely codeword for the atonement of sin and, in this instance, actually signifies the blessing of God. He concluded that judgment was a means to the Day of the Lord but did not signify the Day of the Lord by itself. God's judgment, which will find its climax in the tribulation, will allow Christ's millennial reign. Thus, Mayhue held that Christ's reign will result in blessing.[72] On the contrary, as Helyer argued, the issue with the false teachers, as described by Peter, was their denial not of the goodness of God, but of his justice. They apparently held an apathetic attitude toward the holiness of God and his expectations of his people. Helyer

---

70 Thiede, "Pagan Reader of 2 Peter," 91.
71 Bauckham, *Jude, 2 Peter*, 299.
72 Mayhue, "Day of the Lord," 241.

wrote, "In short, God the Father is both a judging and saving God. The false teachers gravely err by denying the former."[73]

Bauckham argued that since God is Creator and decreed judgment in the past, in which he kept his promises by fulfilling them in destruction, the readers could confidently trust that the judgment that God decreed in this instance against impious men is a reliable promise, since by his own word he made the promise by decree.[74] This view also includes the complete destruction by conflagration, τεθησαυρισμένοι εἰσὶν πυρὶ (are being reserved for fire), as a result of the Father's divine decree of judgment. For an alternate view, G. Z. Heide argued that the condemnation and judgment of God will not be a re-creation ex nihilo via conflagration. Rather, he purported, ". . . the creation in which we now live has a future. Though its future state may result from a process similar to what we expect for our resurrected bodies (Phil. 3:20–21), it nonetheless will be a transformation and renewal rather than a recreation ex nihilo."[75]

The use of νῦν (present) with οὐρανοὶ καὶ ἡ γῆ (heavens and the earth) shows Peter's view that the earth and heavens, as his readers knew them, would not exist in the same way in the future. Rather, Peter indeed purported a re-creation ex nihilo. Therefore, according to Peter, God the Father, who decreed judgment, intends to destroy the heavens and the earth, but implied is a patience on the part of the Father, as evidenced by τηρούμενοι (held). God has not only marked the ἀσεβῶν ἀνθρώπων (impious men) as τηρούμενοι (held) for judgment, but the text implies with the usage of τεθησαυρισμένοι εἰσὶν πυρὶ τηρούμενοι (are being reserved for fire, held) that he also exercises patience. Even the Father's decree of judgment demonstrates his patience.

Peter implied that it is within the full power of the Father to destroy evil without warning. However, the Father often chooses as an integral part of his character to issue a judgment that also may act as a warning, and thereby an offering of merciful patience. Paul J. Achtemeier commented, "God's patience is probably to be understood as the reason why God has delayed, even if not for long, his final judgment, enduring for a time the evil of the contemporary society that opposes him in the form of opposing the Christian community."[76] In this way, Peter described the Father as holding a distinct role that includes judgment in the form of a divine decree involving patience, which is consistent with God's character. While the Son certainly

---

73 Helyer, *Life and Witness of Peter*, 223.
74 Bauckham, *Jude, 2 Peter*, 299.
75 Heide, "New Heaven and the New Earth," 55.
76 Achtemeier, *First Peter*, 263.

will come in judgment in the last times, it will be to do the will of the Father, who has already decreed it.

> 2 Peter 3:12: προσδοκῶντας καὶ σπεύδοντας τὴν παρουσίαν τῆς τοῦ θεοῦ ἡμέρας, δι' ἣν οὐρανοὶ πυρούμενοι λυθήσονται καὶ στοιχεῖα καυσούμενα τήκεται.
>
> looking for and hastening the coming of the Day of God, because of which the heavens will be destroyed and the elements will be consumed by intense heat.

Concerning τῆς τοῦ θεοῦ ἡμέρας (the Day of God), Bauckham noted rightly that this phrase is a very "... unusual ... expression[, as] 'the Day of God,' [is] in place of the normal 'the Day of the Lord.' [The Apocalypse of Peter] ... has 'the day of God,' but is probably dependent on this passage. Revelation 16:14 also has τῆς μεγάλης ἡμέρας τοῦ θεοῦ τοῦ παντοκράτορος, 'the great Day of God the Almighty.'"[77] Ultimately, Bauckham concluded that the author of 2 Peter possibly took his expression from Revelation 16:14. However, depending on the date of composition, namely, if Peter wrote 2 Peter, it would not have been possible for Peter to rely on Revelation, since his death likely took place before the accepted composition date of Revelation. Bratcher noted that "the day of God is the same as the day of the Lord in verse 10 ... the day when God will judge the world."[78] While Peter clearly emphasized the judgment of the whole world, he also showed the distinction between the Son and the Father in this passage.

While the Son will come exercising the end of the decree of judgment, the Father, who has given the decree, will also be present. Davids believed this was the thrust of the usage of τῆς τοῦ θεοῦ ἡμέρας (the Day of God), writing, "The day of judgment can be called the 'day of God' (3:12), not just the 'day of the Lord' or some similar term. That places God at the end of the age as he was the Creator at the beginning."[79] When one looks closely at the christological themes of 2 Peter, especially in apposition to his distinct portrayal of the Son from the Father, one sees that Peter intentionally used themes such as the Father's role as Creator in connection to his role as Judge and Condemner.

With 3:12, τῆς τοῦ θεοῦ ἡμέρας (the Day of God), looking back to 3:10, ἡμέρα κυρίου (Day of the Lord), Peter also insinuated the judgment of God, communicating that on the Day of the Lord, or the Day of God in verse 12, all of one's works "will be made visible." Helmut von Lenhard argued that

---

77 Bauckham, *Jude, 2 Peter*, 325.
78 Bratcher, *Translator's Guide*, 164.
79 Davids, *Theology of James, Peter, and Jude*, 234.

the meaning of God's judgment is not judgment at all, but responsibility. He wrote, "The entire visible world is passing away, but man just needs to deal responsibly before God."[80] However, in light of the previous exposition concerning the judgment of God, this seems unlikely.

J. W. Roberts also offered variant possibilities.[81] Albert M. Wolters added, "Whether or not this proposed technical sense of the passive of heuriskō can be substantiated, it seems clear that the reading heurethesetai in 2 Pet. 3:10 is not only the best-attested text, indirectly supported by two second-century patristic allusions, but also yields excellent sense in its context."[82] R. Larry Overstreet discussed a textual variant related to 2 Peter 3:10, and whether the text should read that God's judgment will culminate so that the earth "shall be burned up" (εὑρεθήσεται) or "shall be found" (εὑρίσκω).[83] Overstreet concluded that there will be "an annihilation after the millennium and a re-creation of the universe is what Peter is here teaching."[84]

Therefore, due to the complete conflagration promised by the Father, Peter clearly presented the Father as Judge in his distinct role, which completes his special role as Creator. Peter emphasized the Father's role as divine Magistrate, and the Son's role as equally divine yet willfully and joyfully obedient to the will of the Father. The Son carries out the will of the Father, but the Father exercises a certain sovereignty over his creation in a distinct and complementary way.

THE FATHER AS DELIVERER

Lastly, Peter not only presented the Father as Preeminent Author and divine Magistrate, but he also described the Father as Deliverer. For a letter written, as Kruger suggested, at such an early period, the letter holds a clear Christology and a distinctive portrayal of the Trinity. While Peter described Jesus, the Son, also as σωτήρ (Savior), he described the Father in terms of his acts and character of deliverance. While Peter certainly emphasized the Father's role as Deliverer, he did this in balance with the Father's role as divine Magistrate who judges and condemns. J. Ramsey Michaels wrote, "If 2 Peter holds in delicate balance the threat of judgment and the hope of mercy, 1 Peter is preoccupied with mercy and salvation. [The] readers . . . have no reason to fear because Christ has won the decisive victory on their

---

80 Author's translation; Lenhard, "Beitrag zur Übersetzung," 129.
81 Roberts, "Note on the Meaning," 32.
82 Wolters, "Worldview," 412.
83 Overstreet, "Study of 2 Peter 3:10–13," 368.
84 Overstreet, "Study of 2 Peter 3:10–13," 368.

behalf by his resurrection and journey to heaven; their baptism is the token of their participation in that victory."[85] Peter's emphasis on deliverance was not out of place in 2 Peter; rather, his emphasis on judgment was not a key aspect of 1 Peter. While the weight of 2 Peter lies with his judgment and consequences for the impious, both letters stress God's amazing saving power.

Peter proved the Father's desire for deliverance for his readers by using narratives that were familiar to those also familiar with the Septuagint. The book *Interpreting the New Testament*, edited by David Alan Black and David S. Dockery, recorded, "That the situation behind 2 Peter calls for a unique response is shown by the presence of Noah and Lot as midrashic types of God's merciful deliverance. The syntax of 2 Peter 2:4–10 clarifies the proper sense in which Lot is dikaios: 'If God . . . rescued Lot . . . , who was vexed . . . , then he knows how to rescue' (vv.4–9)."[86] Subtly, yet clearly, Peter pointed to God's merciful deliverance in 2 Peter. The emphasis of God's mercy in the epistle rests upon the Father's divine role as Patient Promise-Keeper (3:9, 15), Savior (2:4–9), and Preserver (2:5; 3:6).

The Father as Patient Promise-Keeper

First, Peter showed that the Father is a Patient Promise-Keeper. The previous sections focused on the Father's distinction from the Son in Peter's portrayal of his promise-keeping in terms of his divine judgment and condemnation. Intertwined, however, the author intended to show the Father as complete in his character. To this end, the author described the Father also as keeping his promises positively, and he portrayed him as acting patiently with humans. He specifically tied God's patience to his promise concerning the Son's return. Callan commented that "2 Peter . . . explains the delay in Jesus' return as a result of the different meaning of time for God and for humans and as an opportunity for repentance."[87]

Peter's portrayal of the Father's patience was consistent with the Old Testament's portrayal of him. Peter would disagree, therefore, with one who claims that the Old Testament portrayed God as a God of justice and wrath and the New Testament portrayed God as a God of mercy and love. Bauckham wrote, "Jewish tradition also regarded the period before the Flood as a period in which God delayed judgment to give men time for repentance."[88]

---

85 Michaels, *First Peter*, 201.
86 Black and Dockery, eds., *Interpreting the New Testament*, 445.
87 Callan, *Origins of Christian Faith*, 52.
88 Bauckham, *Jude, 2 Peter*, 251.

The following descriptions of the Father depict God as consistent in his character as not only a just Magistrate but also as patient and merciful.

Exegetical Exposition of 2 Peter 3:9, 15

> 2 Peter 3:9: οὐ βραδύνει κύριος τῆς ἐπαγγελίας, ὥς τινες βραδύτητα ἡγοῦνται, ἀλλὰ μακροθυμεῖ εἰς ὑμᾶς, μὴ βουλόμενός τινας ἀπολέσθαι ἀλλὰ πάντας εἰς μετάνοιαν χωρῆσαι.

> The Lord does not delay the promise, as some regard delay, but is patient toward you, not willing that any should perish but that all should go on to repentance.

Peter began 3:9 emphatically with the negative particle opening his statement οὐ βραδύνει (does not delay). Here, κύριος (Lord) could refer to the Son, since the Son is the one who will return physically in the eschaton. However, more likely in this passage, the emphasis is on the Father. The Father, whom Peter presented as Ruler of Time in the context of the epistle, would naturally be the one controlling the punctuality of his promises, as Robert L. Webb and Duane F. Watson implied.[89]

Luke included Peter as one of the witnesses of the last promise of Jesus' Parousia prior to the New Testament church. Acts records, "And while they were gazing into heaven as he went, behold, two men stood by them in white robes, and said, 'Men of Galilee, why do you stand looking into heaven? This Jesus, who was taken up from you into heaven, will come in the same way as you saw him go into heaven'" (Acts 1:10–11, ESV). Likely, as the two heavenly messengers appear to be from the Father, and while τῆς ἐπαγγελίας (the promise) is guaranteed certainly by the Trinity, the Father played a special role in issuing and proclaiming τῆς ἐπαγγελίας (the promise) of Parousia in Acts, and by inference in this passage. Lewis R. Donelson added, "The delay, which is not a delay, results not simply from the differences between human and divine time but also from the character of God."[90] The emphatic opening emphasizes that βραδύνει (does delay) actually is a myth.[91] The phrase ὥς τινες βραδύτητα ἡγοῦνται (as some regard delay) refers to the false teachers, who apparently felt that the Father had delayed his promise of Parousia. The words βραδύνει (does delay) and βραδύτητα (delay) have a nuanced meaning depending on the context. Witherington argued:

---

89 Webb and Watson, *Reading Second Peter*, 55.
90 Donelson, *1 and 2 Peter*, 212.
91 Schreiner, *1, 2 Peter, Jude*, 394.

In 2 Peter 3:9 we have the verb *bradyon*, which means 'is slow in effecting, is delayed or late,' or 'is negligent about.' Since, however, the problem is lateness (i.e., the parousia is late and overdue), not slowness, the latter two translations better suit the context. But how can God be late for the messianic banquet of which he is the host and scheduler? In this verse, then, the author is denying that God is late or overdue (or slow). Lateness presupposes a knowledge of when the end should have happened, definitely, and the author is going on to point out that no human has that sort of inside information.[92]

Therefore, the likely interpretation is "lateness." However, "delay" is preferable because it is an accurate definition of both βραδύνει and βραδύτητα, and it does not interpret the text itself, but allows the context to show itself to the reader. Bauckham supported this view, writing, "V8 [shows] God cannot be confined to human ideas of lateness. He does not explicitly face the issue of the alleged time-limit in the prophecy of the Parousia, but simply denies that the delay in fulfillment means that there will be no fulfillment. [God is] sovereign over the time of the End, and defers it in his own good purpose."[93] Peter's usage of the word was the idea of delay, but he certainly wanted to point out that the idea that the false teachers had, namely, that the Parousia was late, was false.

In a positive Petrine twist, that which the false teachers interpreted as delay, βραδύνει/βραδύτητα, was actually the Father's patience and mercy, ἀλλὰ μακροθυμεῖ εἰς ὑμᾶς (but is patient toward you), on those very same critics and his desire for their repentance, μὴ βουλόμενός τινας ἀπολέσθαι ἀλλὰ πάντας εἰς μετάνοιαν χωρῆσαι (not willing that any should perish but that all should go on to repentance).[94]

Peter presented the Father as directing time. In this timeline, he does not rule as an amoral dictator, but he exercises judgment and condemnation while simultaneously exercising patience. The idea that the Father is patient does not only find representation in 2 Peter, but it begins in the Old Testament narrative. Bauckham pointed out:

> The idea of God's 'forbearance' ('longsuffering, patience' μακροθυμία) derives from the OT description of God as 'slow to anger' in Exodus 34:6, the central OT revelation of God's character, and the numerous passages which echo that text (Num. 14:18; Neh. 9:17; Pss. 86:15 [LXX 85 :15]: 103:8 [LXX 102:8];

---

92 Witherington, *Indelible Image*, 414.
93 Bauckham, *Jude, 2 Peter*, 311.
94 Bauckham, *Jude, 2 Peter*, 327.

145:8 [LZZ 144:8]; Joel 1:13; Jonah 4:2; Nah 1:3;Wis 15:1: in all these verses the LXX translation is μακρόθυμος 'forbearing'. It is that quality by which God bears with sinners, holds back his wrath, refrains from intervening in judgment as soon as the sinner's deeds deserve it, though not indefinitely (cf. 4 Ezra 7:33; Sir 5:4–7). In Jewish theology it has strongly chronological implication (Strobel, *Untersuchungen*, 31): God's forbearance creates an interval, a period of respite, while judgment is deferred and a last opportunity for repentance is allowed.[95]

The Father does this in a self-written narrative that only he decrees. Webb and Watson wrote, "There is a movement from God the creator to God the patient redeemer to God the re-creator of a world suitable for the redeemed."[96] Webb and Watson did not argue that God somehow changed in his character. However, they argued that God acted in these ways specifically to bring about his divine narrative. Therefore, Peter's Christology purported that the Son, equally God (1:1) and authoritative (Matt 28:19), subjects his will to, fulfills the decrees of, and keeps the promises of the Father.

Peter described the Father in his distinct role as a Patient Promise-Keeper. Regardless of the outcome, whether positive or negative for the one receiving the promise, he will keep his promise. When the Father decrees divine judgment, his character demands that he also shows mercy, as Peter showed in this verse as he emphasized the Father's patience, which the false teachers interpreted as a delay causing him to be late.

Peter presented the Father as trustworthy in general and also specifically in regard to prophecy, which he inspired in the Old Testament period. Himes wrote:

> In 2 Peter the emphasis on fulfillment becomes the main line of argument against the opponents: fulfilled prophecy is a co-testament with eye-witnessed revelation concerning Christ. Otherwise there would hardly be any contrast between true prophecy and false prophecy. Furthermore, even prophecy which has not yet come to pass is certain eventually to occur (note especially 2 Peter 3 and the issue of the delayed Parousia). Thus, a holistic look at Petrine theology reveals that the concept of fulfillment is a necessary part of prophecy. Indeed, prophecy without fulfillment is not true prophecy.[97]

---

95 Bauckham, *Jude, 2 Peter*, 312.
96 Webb and Watson, *Reading Second Peter*, 55.
97 Himes, "Peter and the Prophetic Word," 240.

The appearance of delay represents God's grace on display and his desire for the impious ones to repent.

The word πάντας (all) has represented a roadblock for some interpreters. For instance, the Fayumic text does not claim that God wants all to come to repentance. Rather, it specifically calls out the opponents in the letter to repent. It seems that the scribes intentionally changed the wording of the text. Whereas in Western culture it is offensive to many people that God would not save everyone, it was apparently offensive in many cultures, as in the world that produced the Fayumic text, that God would want to save everyone. While one culture's optimistic worldview sees mankind as generally good, other worldviews tend to be pessimistic generally in terms of the goodness of men, which one observes in the Fayumic text. Therefore, in order to diminish the offense of the idea that God wants to save everyone, ἀλλὰ πάντας εἰς μετάνοιαν χωρῆσαι (but that all should go on to repentance), the Fayumic text has narrowed the scope to include only the false teachers. Interestingly, the Fayumic text at least recognizes that the Father wants to save impious people and offer them opportunities for repentance.[98] Logically, he would also want to save other impious people. If so, no reason is implied why he would only desire to save one group and not the other group.

This verse has been a source of discussion in the debate between Reformed theologians and theologians espousing a variety of other views. Interestingly, Douglas Welker Kennard took a completely different approach and called into question the Petrine understanding of salvation and redemption, writing, "In Peter, one can be soteriologically redeemed without having been saved. Furthermore, while Peter includes redemption with the total process of salvation he indicates by the extent of redemption that the redemption of an individual does not guarantee that he shall be ultimately saved."[99] Basic hermeneutical rules determine that the clearest meaning of the text is likely the correct interpretation. The Fayumic text forced a textual change in order to come to a different interpretation. Kennard called into question the entire Petrine understanding of salvation and redemption as a conclusion of his difficulty in interpreting what he viewed to be a difficult passage. No credible reason exists to reinterpret an otherwise clear passage.

Surely, the mystery of God shows itself in this passage. Because God is eternal, he does not work on a human timeline and is able to perceive time as wholly other than Peter's readers, he is able to act as sovereign Judge, condemn sin, and provide repentance, without contradiction. However, the patience God exercises does not last forever. As Bauckham noted, "There can

---

98 Blumenthal, "Hoffnung für die Gegner?" 135.
99 Kennard, "Petrine Redemption," 401.

be no presuming on the Lord's patience (cf. Rom 2:4). The persistently unrepentant will find that judgment comes unexpectedly soon (v 10a)."[100] The Father still desires that all would come to repentance because of his character, while fully knowing the future that all will not come to repentance. Peter did not see this as a contradiction, but as something beautiful that exists specifically in the Father's character. Duane F. Watson and Terrance Callan added, "God is patient, wanting all to repent (v. 9)."[101] Webb and Watson added:

> [Peter] assumes that the world is wicked and his group is faithful. God will bring judgement upon the wicked and reward to the faithful. God has a plan to execute both by burning the current heavens and earth with fire and replacing them with new ones that the faithful will share as part of their eschatological reward. This plan was revealed in part by the judgment of the flood and the promise of fire. God's plan is tempered by the divine desire for as many people to repent as possible, and God's plan will be consummated suddenly and without warning.[102]

Thus, God is the Creator of all who sustains in existence all that he has created until the time appointed for its dissolution. The Father, Peter implied, is not like other Hellenistic/pagan deities, who ruled only with an iron fist. In his omnipotence, his desire to deliver impious people exists, even while his desire for justice and righteousness never wanes. Karl A. Kuhn held the position that "God's mercy subverts rigid categories and confident expectations of who will and will not be counted among the faithful. The letter-writer ... grapples with the age-old tension between God's judgment and tremendous mercy (see, e.g., Exod. 34:6–7)."[103]

According to 2 Peter, because the Father is a Patient Promise-Keeper, it proves his desire to deliver people from sin. His desire is so enormous, and his mercy so great, that he is even able to desire deeply that everyone would come to repentance, regardless of whether everyone will repent. God, therefore, is the Deliverer of the entire world and all are partakers of his common grace, but specifically he is the Deliverer of those who repent toward him and experience salvific grace, which he desires for everyone. The Father willed his desire, which he also shares with the Son. Out of this same desire, the Son faced death on a cross. Peter presented the Son's work as a direct outcome of the desire of the Father. The Gospel of Luke records, "Father, if you are willing, remove this cup from me. Nevertheless, not my will, but

---

100 Bauckham, *Jude, 2 Peter*, 313.
101 Watson and Callan, *First and Second Peter*, 212.
102 Webb and Watson, *Reading Second Peter*, 53.
103 Kuhn, "2 Peter 3:1–3," 312.

yours, be done" (Luke 22:42, ESV). The Son did not go to the cross purely by his own will, although he shared the desire, but he did it by the will of the Father. Peter's Christology not only included Jesus as the divine Savior, but he showed the Father to direct the Son through his will, expressing his own desire for all to come to repentance.

> 2 Peter 3:15: καὶ τὴν τοῦ κυρίου ἡμῶν μακροθυμίαν σωτηρίαν ἡγεῖσθε, καθὼς καὶ ὁ ἀγαπητὸς ἡμῶν ἀδελφὸς Παῦλος κατὰ τὴν δοθεῖσαν αὐτῷ σοφίαν ἔγραψεν ὑμῖν.
>
> and regard the patience of our Lord as salvation, just as also our beloved brother Paul wrote to you according to the wisdom given him.

Peter continued in 3:15 to make the argument of 3:9. He reiterated his statement that the Lord did not delay, but he offered patience, a period for repentance to the end of salvation. With Peter's mention of Paul, he did not limit his argument to his own knowledge or inspiration. Just as Peter recognized Paul's writings, some with which he was familiar at the time of composition of 2 Peter, as inspired Scripture on the level of the Old Testament prophets, he also mentioned Paul in conjunction with the Father's patience. The New Testament presents God's patience in the Pauline Epistles. Albert E. Barnett noted, "[It] seems to represent a development from Romans 2:4. The delay of the Parousia is explained in terms of God's patience and . . . desire that men repent. This is Paul's explanation of the delay of impending judgment. This idea is expressed in the New Testament only in Romans 2:4, 9:22, and 2 Peter 3:15 (cf. 1 Pet. 3:20)."[104]

Likely, Peter and Paul were in Rome together and possibly this was something they discussed. Kruger wrote, "We see how God is μακροθυμεῖ (longsuffering) so that all may come to repentance in 2 Peter 3:9, 15 and how the gospel was preached in 1 Peter 3:20 to those in the days of Noah when God's μακροθυμία (longsuffering) waited. These intimate connections can hardly be attributed to any sort of pseudonymous author."[105] D. E. Hiebert added:

> That Peter and the other apostles maintained an active interest in the missionary activities of Paul is obvious. Bigg boldly declares that it is 'probably that St. Peter received every one of St. Paul's Epistles within a month or two of its publication.' It is known that Paul's letters were held in high esteem by Christians and scrutinized with great care by friends and foes alike (2 Cor. 10:10; 2 Thess. 2:2; Rom. 3:8). That his epistles were readily

---

104 Barnett, *Paul Becomes a Literary Influence*, 225.
105 Kruger, "Authenticity of 2 Peter," 660.

circulated among the churches shortly after their composition is clear (cf. Col. 4:16).[106]

Therefore, this specific idea of God's patience in the Petrine and Pauline corpus represents a unique teaching within the New Testament.

Peter mentioned Paul in order to strengthen his position with his readers. Many of whom likely had become skeptics of prophecy were now challenged by Peter as to what constitutes true prophecy. Peter presented his Christology, and here the distinct roles played by the Father and Son, as divinely inspired truths, not prophecies that he concocted on his own. The Father, the Mover of Men, by means of the Holy Spirit saw fit that Peter would present the ideas they received. He affirmed Paul as a mouthpiece of inspiration, but he did this in direct opposition to the false teachers, who also claimed prophecy. In this passage, Peter emphasized that his truth about the Father came from the Father himself, as did Paul's. The false teachers received their pseudoprophecy elsewhere, likely from the Epicureans, many of whom had infiltrated churches and syncretized their beliefs in the early church period, according to G. L. Green.[107] However, in Petrine fashion, he presented the Father as Patient Promise-Keeper even towards those whom he considerd impious. Kuhn noted, ". . . [The Father] is holding out for all people's embrace of salvation, including even those horrendously reprobate false teachers (see Rom 2:4; 11:32; 1 Tim 2:4)."[108] As a patient God who desires to deliver all, the Father even promised the worst of the false teachers deliverance, via a period of patience that he designed, so that all might repent, ultimately accomplished through the Son's unique work.

The Father as Savior

Peter also presented the Father as Savior. This role is not unique to the Father. The Son also actively saves, as does the Holy Spirit. However, in 2 Peter 2:4–9, Peter showed specifically the role the Father played in salvation history and continues to embody in his character.

---

106 Hiebert, "Selected Studies," 334.
107 Green, "Prophecies," 117.
108 Kuhn, "2 Peter 3:1–3," 312.

Exegetical Exposition of 2 Peter 2:4–9

2 Peter 2:4–9; Εἰ γὰρ ὁ θεὸς ἀγγέλων ἁμαρτησάντων οὐκ ἐφείσατο, ἀλλὰ σειραῖς ζόφου ταρταρώσας παρέδωκεν εἰς κρίσιν τηρουμένους, καὶ ἀρχαίου κόσμου οὐκ ἐφείσατο, ἀλλὰ ὄγδοον Νῶε δικαιοσύνης κήρυκα ἐφύλαξεν, κατακλυσμὸν κόσμῳ ἀσεβῶν ἐπάξας, καὶ πόλεις Σοδόμων καὶ Γομόρρας τεφρώσας καταστροφῇ κατέκρινεν, ὑπόδειγμα μελλόντων ἀσεβέσιν τεθεικώς, καὶ δίκαιον Λὼτ καταπονούμενον ὑπὸ τῆς τῶν ἀθέσμων ἐν ἀσελγείᾳ ἀναστροφῆς ἐρρύσατο, βλέμματι γὰρ καὶ ἀκοῇ ὁ δίκαιος ἐγκατοικῶν ἐν αὐτοῖς ἡμέραν ἐξ ἡμέρας ψυχὴν δικαίαν ἀνόμοις ἔργοις ἐβασάνιζεν, καὶ δίκαιον Λὼτ καταπονούμενον ὑπὸ τῆς τῶν ἀθέσμων ἐν ἀσελγείᾳ ἀναστροφῆς ἐρρύσατο, βλέμματι γὰρ καὶ ἀκοῇ ὁ δίκαιος ἐγκατοικῶν ἐν αὐτοῖς ἡμέραν ἐξ ἡμέρας ψυχὴν δικαίαν ἀνόμοις ἔργοις ἐβασάνιζεν, οἶδεν κύριος εὐσεβεῖς ἐκ πειρασμοῦ ῥύεσθαι, ἀδίκους δὲ εἰς ἡμέραν κρίσεως κολαζομένους τηρεῖν.

For if God did not spare the angels when they sinned, but cast them into Tartarus and committed them to chains of gloomy darkness, held back until the judgment, and if he did not spare the ancient world, but preserved eight, including Noah, a proclaimer of righteousness, when he brought a flood upon the world of the impious, and if by reducing the cities of Sodom and Gomorrah to ashes, He condemned them to destruction, making them an example of what is going to happen to the impious, and if He rescued righteous Lot, worn down by the licentious behavior of the lawless, he saw and heard the righteous man, living among them, day by day his righteous soul tormented by their lawless deeds, then the Lord knows how to deliver the pious from trials, and to hold the unrighteous under punishment until the Day of Judgment.

In these verses, Peter gave his readers a familiar history lesson, while using the narrative to emphasize the Father's faithfulness by means of his salvation. While the epistle calls the Son, Jesus, the Savior in the opening verses, in these verses Peter looked to the past, emphasizing the work of the Father in order to demonstrate to his readers that the Father is a great Deliverer as he evidenced on many occasions. Peter employed a series of phrases and comparisons.

First, beginning with a series of conditional statements, Peter wrote, "if God did not spare the angels." He cited their sin as the reason the Father did not spare them. Peter tells the readers that the angels were "cast into Tartarus and committed to chains of gloomy darkness." Peter did not employ syncretism. Spiros Zodhiates wrote, "These angels are being held in this netherworld dungeon until the day of final judgment. Peter's usage of this term is not evidence either that Christianity was a syncretistic religion or that Peter himself believed in the pagan myths about Tartarus. Peter has adapted a word and not adopted a theology."[109] The use of the word ταρταρώσας (Tartarus) in 2:4 is a hapax legomenon and Peter employed it here with precision. Peter literally told his readers the angels are in ταρταρώσας (Tartarus). John H. Elliot wrote, "According to Greek cosmology, Tartarus was a subterranean place below Hades where evil people were committed and punished after death. Use of this term in 2 Peter represents still another instance of the author's blending of Jewish and Greek worldviews."[110] However, as Zodhiates noted, he likely borrowed an idea common to his readers and redefined it. Possibly, for his audience this was clearer. The use of the word communicated the exact idea he wanted to communicate. Peter's use of the word is comparable to the English phrase "the pit of hell." Preachers use this phrase emphatically, but they do not imply thereby that there is an actual pit of hell. Rather, it is idiomatic expression.

Second, Peter wrote, "if the Father did not spare the ancient world." The author used the first and second conditional statements to emphasize the majesty of the salvation the Father provides. Callan wrote, "[Verse 5] cites the precedent of the flood, '[If God] did not spare the ancient world'. This obviously provided another precedent for God's punishment of evildoers. However, it also allowed 2 Peter to introduce antecedent for God's salvation of the righteous, i.e., the salvation of Noah and his family."[111] The text records that the Father "preserved eight, including Noah, a proclaimer of righteousness." Noah apparently was a theme very important to Peter. Kruger wrote:

> 2 Peter speaks of how Noah was delivered from the flood (2 Pet. 2:5) and how the earth was formerly destroyed by water (2 Pet. 3:6–7). We see this theme also in 1 Peter 3:19–21 when it is said that Christ preached to those who disobeyed in the days of Noah. There is an interesting connection to note here. 2 Peter 2:5 describes Noah as a κήρυκα ("preacher") of righteousness which is the only place in the New Testament where Noah is described as such. In 1 Peter 3:19 we see the fact that Christ went and ἐκήρυξεν ("preached") to those in Noah's day. If one understands this text in 1 Peter as Christ preaching through

---

109 Zodhiates, *Word Study Dictionary*, s.v. "ταρταρόω."
110 Elliot, *Augsburg Commentary*, 148.
111 Callan, "Use of Jude by Second Peter," 50.

"Noah," then we have an amazing correlation between the two epistles.[112]

Peter's Christology and its impact on New Testament believers fulfilled his view of the Old Testament. Noah provided a visual portrayal of salvation. Peter painted a picture of a Father and Son who are both actively involved in salvation, yet throughout history, while unified, have held different roles. Clearly, Peter did not describe Jesus, the Son, as the one who condemned some and saved others. However, if Kruger is correct, the Father preached righteousness through Noah, directed by the Holy Spirit. One observes that Peter's understanding of the Trinity, and more specifically the distinction between the Father and the Son, was vividly clear. Clearly, Peter cited Noah's righteousness, not sinless perfection, as the reason he and his family received salvation. The Father saved those whom he believed were righteous, and he did not save those who were impious. By implication, Noah, a preacher of righteousness, found salvation by the faith that he had in a vessel of salvation the Father provided just at the opportune time. While the ark provided physical salvation, Noah's personal faith in the Father and his deliverance ultimately provided his eternal salvation.

Third, Peter wrote the conditional statement "if by reducing the cities of Sodom and Gomorrah to ashes." Peter told his readers that God destroyed Sodom and Gomorrah and made the people there an example of how God deals with the impious. In apposition, 2 Peter mentions Lot as evidence for the Father's history of saving. The Father considered Lot, who also did not live a life of sinless perfection, as righteous. Upon this basis, the Father graciously removed him from the physical destruction of the twin cities. Peter wrote that the Father rescued, ἐρρύσατο, Lot. The text portrays Lot as someone who lived in the middle of sin, yet the Father rescued him in spite of the situation in which he found himself. Michael Green noted:

> No temptation from within or test from without is too great to be endured, for God not only regulates it, but gives His people the strength to face it (1 Cor. 10:13). Note that God delivers a man 'out of' (*ek*) not 'away from' (*apo*) trials. Christianity is no insurance policy against the trials of life. God allows them to befall the Christian; He meets us in them and delivers us out of them.[113]

The Father knew Lot's most inward thoughts and rescued him, as evidenced by his great distress that wore him down, καταπονούμενον ὑπὸ τῆς τῶν ἀθέσμων ἐν ἀσελγείᾳ ἀναστροφῆς (worn down by the licentious

---

112 Kruger, "Authenticity of 2 Peter," 660.
113 Green, *Second Peter*, 102.

behavior). Concerning Lot, Peter noted βλέμματι γὰρ καὶ ἀκοῇ ὁ δίκαιος ... ἐβασάνιζεν (he saw and heard the righteous man, tormented). While Lot's outward actions were not always wise or right, he showed his trust of the Father. In contrast, J. Makujina argued that Lot was not the best example for God's salvation of the righteous, and he held that Peter's information of Lot must have come from Jewish lore rather than the Old Testament.[114] However, this view does not fit well with the gospel narrative (ἐπίγνωσις in 2 Peter) throughout the New Testament, which is not a story of people who were saved by means of their own righteousness, but rather of people who were saved by grace, declared righteous as a result of their knowledge of, and trust in, God, who is himself righteous. One sees the seriousness of Lot's faith especially when compared to the narrative of his wife, who almost escaped the wicked cities. Even in the midst of some of the most wicked cities ever to exist on earth, the Father showed his great love and mercy through the salvation of those whom he saw were righteous.

Peter ended the series of conditional statements with a twofold compliment. First, he wrote, "Then the Lord knows how to deliver the pious from trials." Bratcher commented, "This is the conclusion of the series of 'if' clauses beginning at verse 4: 'All of this shows (or, proves) that the Lord knows how'. Here the Lord is God."[115] Therefore, the thrust of these verses first ends with the compliment that gives hope to believers. Those who truly trust the Father in their hearts that he will also provide a way of physical salvation via Christ's work and return will also find rescue in the sure salvation of the Father eternally and spiritually through the Son, as the Father demonstrated with Noah and Lot by means of the ark and the escape from Sodom and Gomorrah. Initially upon hearing this, this may have also brought hope to the false teachers, who felt that inwardly they too were righteous. Bauckham wrote, "This verse is the apodosis of the long conditional sentence verses 4–10a. Putting the lesson concerning the righteous first enables the writer to end emphatically with the lesson concerning the wicked, applied to his opponents."[116] Peter ended with a reaffirmation of the surety of their eventual destruction, barring repentance. In the end, the Father offers hope even to the false teachers if they only repent. Once again, the seriousness of God's justice and wrath is not contrary to his nature as Savior, Rescuer, and great Deliverer. While the Father promises to judge and condemn those who are impious, he also promises to save those who are

---

114 Makujina, "Lot in 2 Peter," 255.
115 Bratcher, *Translator's Guide*, 150.
116 Bauckham, *Jude, 2 Peter*, 253.

pious in faith in him, which Peter presented as also including the promises and truths about his Son Jesus.

The Father as Preserver

As divine Deliverer, 2 Peter presents the Father as Preserver. Specifically, he preserves and protects people who belong to him in faith. Peter showed Jesus to be the Master Redeemer who died for the sin of mankind, securing the basis for eternal salvation. The New Testament also called the Holy Spirit the Sealer of Faith (Eph 4:30). The Father uniquely has the role of preserving people for salvation who are pious whom he also desires to deliver. One key theme in the epistle describes the preservation the Father provides.

Exegetical Exposition of 2 Peter 2:5; 3:6

> 2 Peter 2:5: καὶ ἀρχαίου κόσμου οὐκ ἐφείσατο, ἀλλὰ ὄγδοον Νῶε δικαιοσύνης κήρυκα ἐφύλαξεν, κατακλυσμὸν κόσμῳ ἀσεβῶν ἐπάξας.
> and if he did not spare the ancient world, but preserved eight, including Noah, a proclaimer of righteousness, when he brought a flood upon the world of the impious.
>
> 2 Peter 3:6: δι' ὧν ὁ τότε κόσμος ὕδατι κατακλυσθεὶς ἀπώλετο.
> through which the world at that time was destroyed being flooded by water.

In apposition to God's dealings with Noah in 2:5, the Father destroyed the ancient world in 3:6. Peter not only demonstrated the Father's saving power, which the Son also exhibits in his character as the Second Person of the Trinity in his work on the cross, but Peter showed that the Father is the author of preservation. He provides vessels, both physical and spiritual, that protect and preserve his people in real, practical, and meaningful ways. While the word preservation is not present in 2:5 or 3:6, the common picture that Peter painted for his readers is of the ark. Many scholars have noted this imagery, its impact upon Peter's readers, and its application for Christians today. Bauckham noted, "Noah, preserved from the old world to be the beginning of the new world after the Flood, is a type of faithful Christians who will be preserved from the present world to inherit the new world after the judgment."[117] The ark represented the Father's grace toward

---

117 Bauckham, *Jude, 2 Peter*, 250.

Noah as he preserved him from judgment, death, destruction, and the antediluvian world in which he lived. Schreiner also noted the imagery and tied it to the Father's preservation of his righteous people denoted by their piety in faith. Schreiner wrote:

> Peter did not focus only on the judgment of the wicked but also the preservation of the righteous. God is the one who preserved and protected (ephlazen) Noah from the judgment. Peter's lesson for his readers is evident. God will protect those who resist the enticements of the false teachers. The faithful will be vindicated by God. Noah was not alone in his righteousness, but he was preserved along with seven others—his wife, his three sons, and their wives.[118]

Simon J. Kistemaker chose to emphasize the Father's great power within his act of preservation, writing, "God, who made the world, also has the power to destroy it. He upholds his creation by his power."[119] Finally, Elliot commented, "God's not sparing either the sinful angels before the Flood or the ancient world during the Flood, is contrasted to his preserving righteous Noah and his family."[120] This subtle mention of the preservation by the Father, yet vivid image of its application, demonstrates Peter's masterful description of one more aspect of the Father as Deliverer in comparison to and in conjunction with the role of the Son.

PETRINE CHRISTOLOGY OF JESUS' UNIQUENESS IN THE NEW TESTAMENT

This chapter has examined the uniqueness of the Son and his distinctness from the Father as Peter presented them as an inimitable paradigm of his broader Christology, examining the ideas, titles, and roles in the text exegetically, expositionally, textually, and circumstantially. At the same time, the author assessed various points of disagreement concerning the uniqueness of the Son, his unity with the Father, and their distinctness, where necessary, and established the shortcomings and strengths of each. Peter demonstrated a consistent and high Christology and distinctly formulated theology in 2 Peter.

First, Peter made it clear in 2 Peter that Jesus is not like other sons of God. Rather, Jesus is the unique Son of God. He portrayed him as the one

---

118 Schreiner, *1, 2 Peter, Jude*, 338.
119 Kistemaker, *Epistles of Peter*, 329.
120 Elliot, *Augsburg Commentary*, 148.

and only Son of God in all of history. Peter presented him as unique in his relationship with the Father, as one yet distinct. The author presented the Son as fully divine and as holding a special role that a godly prophet in the Old Testament did not hold. The epistle only describes one Son as being the Master Redeemer with a special relationship with and ownership over all his people.

On the one hand, Peter was very comfortable in calling Jesus God. He also called him Lord in designating his deity, while holding that he is God's Son. On the other hand, Peter called the Son by his name, Jesus, in other parts of the epistle, and used the word God to refer to the Father. Peter was not confused, and he did not contradict himself. Rather, his letter represents a grand style that he penned very specifically, employing several hapax legomena. His distinction between the Father and the Son was a natural yet calculated description that represented Peter's Christology. Peter placed his description of the work of the Father in careful connection to the work of Christ. He specifically employed a host of descriptions to explain the Father's many roles as the First Person of the Trinity in order to distinguish his work from the Son's, even while both remain of one essence.

Second, the unity yet distinction of the Father and Son in Peter's Christology should come as no surprise to the reader. In the Gospel of Mark, also known as Peter's Gospel, as inferred by Papias 9:2–13, Mark recounted the transfiguration. In Mark 8:29, Peter confessed Jesus as the Christ, yet in 9:2–13 the text speaks of the Son and the Father. That the Messiah was also not only the Son of Man but also the Son of God in the text was remarkable due to the Jewish setting of the event.

Third, Bruce Chilton and Craig Evans argued that in Peter's speech at Pentecost he already held a very clear knowledge of his Christology in relationship to early expressions of the Trinity. Chilton and Evans wrote:

> In Peter's speech at Pentecost, Jesus, having been exalted to the right hand of God, receives the promise of the holy spirit from the father and pours it out on his followers (2:33). The spirit that is poured out, then, comes directly from the majesty of God, from his rule over creation as a whole. This is the spirit as it hovered over the waters at the beginning of creation (Gen 1:1), and not as limited to Israel. Because the spirit is of God, who creates people in the divine image, its presence marks God's own activity, in which all those who follow Jesus are to be included. Jesus' own program had involved proclaiming God's kingdom on the authority of his possession of God's spirit. Now,

as a consequence of the resurrection, Jesus had poured out that same spirit upon those who would follow him.[121]

Peter certainly was comfortable differentiating between the roles of Jesus and the Father in his Christology, while maintaining the belief in one God and the deity of Christ. A short overview of Peter's Christology and its relationship to his understanding of the Godhead shows a man of consistent thought, clear theology, and careful expression.

Fourth, after Peter described Jesus as God the Son in 2 Peter, he described the Father as the Preeminent Author who created all things, rules over all time within his creation, and moves people within his creation creatively and with divine inspiration. He presented the Father as a sovereign King who makes decisions based upon his own divine will and is not subject to any human or angelic being.

Fifth, Peter also exhibited the Father as the divine Magistrate who always keeps his promise to condemn sinners and the impious, and as one whose own history proves this. Peter purported that the Father, as divine Magistrate, is also the one who specifically decrees divine judgment, though this judgment may be implemented by the Son by way of his will within the Godhead.

Lastly, Peter exhibited the distinctness of the Son and the Father by emphasizing the Father's role as divine Deliverer, who simultaneously exhibits his role as Judge and Condemner, but in his character also acts as Patient Promise-Keeper. Because of the Son's work on the cross, which was the will of the Father, Peter presented both God the Father and God the Son as equally divine Savior of all people, marked by their faith in God, not their works. Finally, Peter illustrated that the Father, in his infinite wisdom and love, acts in his role as divine Preserver of his people in unity with God the Son.

---

[121] Chilton and Evans, *Missions of James, Peter, and Paul*, 5.

4

Conclusion

The purpose of this monograph is to examine the Christology of Peter from key texts in 2 Peter. The author chose texts that specifically speak about the divinity of Jesus or his uniqueness, and thus distinctness from God the Father. As with any significant research, other issues often arise that are outside the scope of the work. In this work the author found no less than four areas of future research for other students of the New Testament to examine, including Peter's phraseology in connection to authorship, specific Petrine emphases in comparison to Pauline ones, gospel themes within the Petrine corpus, and the role of amanuenses and pseudepigrapha in the first and second centuries AD.

IMPLICATIONS FOR FURTHER RESEARCH

First, while stylistic differences and implications for authorship in the Petrine Epistles were difficult for scholars to reconcile, Birger A. Pearson noted that there are also similarities, writing, "Finding that there is a greater proportion of shared vocabulary between 1 and 2 Peter, [one] concludes that they were composed by the same author, namely, Peter. Second Peter can indeed be dated to the time of the apostolic church."[1] It would be advantageous for a scholar to make a thorough examination of the specific phrases Peter employed in the epistles that bear his name, and possibly material from Acts and the Gospel narratives.

---

1 Pearson, "James, 1–2 Peter, Jude," 383.

Robert Horton Gundry wrote that the style of 2 Peter "is different than that of 1 Peter; but a difference in amanuenses may account for that. Remarkable similarities of phraseology between 2 Peter and 1 Peter and the Petrine speeches in Acts point to a common source, the Apostle Peter."[2] Did Peter employ an amanuensis, dictating his material? Would his specific phraseology transmit through dictation, while leaving the possibility for varied syntax and style? Such research concerning the phraseology of 2 Peter would answer important questions like these and help scholars make inference as to their impact on the understanding of the viability of Petrine authorship.

Second, 2 Peter's mention of the apostle Paul, at least some of his writings, and his apostolic authority demand a closer look into the themes, emphases, and Christology that 2 Peter and the Pauline corpus exhibit and purport. A possible theme for exploration is the doctrine of inspiration, specifically concerning the roles of the First, Second, and Third Persons of the Trinity.

Third, this work argued that Peter used the term ἐπιγνῶσις (full knowledge) when speaking of what Paul normally called the gospel. According to Larry Helyer, the gospel presents itself quite clearly in 2 Peter. If Peter employed a different term when speaking of the gospel, the epistle deserves a reexamination of the themes associated. Helyer wrote:

> In his salutation, Peter attaches to Jesus Christ the title 'our God and Savior Jesus Christ' (2 Pet. 1:1). Immediately thereafter, in his blessing on the readers, he follows suit with the quintessential New Testament affirmation of faith, 'Jesus our Lord' (2 Pet. 1:2). God, Savior, and Lord are juxtaposed with Jesus Christ, all in the same immediate context. Herein lays the heart of the New Testament gospel.[3]

With this in mind, which gospel themes run throughout 2 Peter? Where is the crimson path that flows through the Bible found in 2 Peter? Käsemann famously claimed that the gospel and the cross do not appear in 2 Peter. However, is the gospel present, and what are the specific gospel themes within 2 Peter itself? How do 2 Peter's gospel themes and implications of the gospel compare to the gospel themes of the New Testament? While this work has shown that Peter held a high Christology in 2 Peter, an examination of the gospel themes within the epistle would contribute to its scope, and would provide yet another perspective on 2 Peter than Käsemann presented.

2 Gundry, *Survey of the New Testament*, 354.
3 Helyer, *Life and Witness*, 217.

Fourth, two areas that could possibly be combined in one study would be the role of amanuenses and the role of pseudepigrapha in the first and second centuries AD. Kermit Titrud wrote:

> Universal doubt [exists] as to whether or not 1 Peter and 2 Peter were written by the same writer. More than likely Peter used different amanuenses for the two letters, or possibly Peter himself wrote 2 Peter whereas 1 Peter was written via Silvanus. The use of amanuenses was common. Paul himself used one in Romans (16:22), and probably in all or most of his epistles (Phil. 19; 1 Cor. 16:21; Gal. 6:11; Col. 4:18; 2 Thess. 3:17). The apostles probably did not dictate word by word to their amanuenses, but more than likely the amanuenses were given a free hand with respect to the grammatical construction of the content dictated to them.[4]

This oft-cited explanation deserves more study. Specifically, a general examination of the use of amanuenses would be helpful in this discussion. How often did authors employ amanuenses? Why did people typically employ amanuenses? Was it an acceptable practice to use an amanuensis? How did others view letters and their contents or authorship, knowing that an author produced a work, possibly by means of dictation, with the help of an amanuensis? In such a study, asking the same questions of pseudepigrapha would provide comparative research that is helpful in assessing the credibility of arguments concerning the authorship of 2 Peter, since often scholars explain stylistic differences between 1 and 2 Peter either by suggesting the use of an amanuensis or asserting that the letter is pseudepigraphal.

While a debate exists among New Testament scholars concerning the authorship of 2 Peter, further study is helpful in making academic conclusions about Petrine Christology. The credibility of the Christology as distinctly Petrine rests upon the premise that Peter wrote 2 Peter. Even with the emphasis on 2 Peter by Terrance Callan, Richard J. Bauckham, and Thomas Schreiner over the last decades, 2 Peter remains one of the least-researched books of the entire New Testament. The lack of research is not due to a lack of material or interesting and important issues. Rather, 2 Peter contains much information pertinent to faith, practice, and New Testament scholarship that is worthy of future study.

---

4 Titrud, "Function of καί," 256.

TOWARD A PETRINE CHRISTOLOGY

Even though this work does not and cannot answer every christological or important question in 2 Peter, it does move the reader to a fuller understanding of Peter's distinct Christology in two areas, and it specifically challenges long-held assumptions by scholarship, as purported by Ernst Käsemann. Käsemann famously stated, "The real theological problem of the epistle we are considering lies in the fact that its eschatology lacks any vestige of Christological orientation."[5] Käsemann, a German New Testament scholar, along with those who followed him, did not argue with his theologically conservative counterparts that 2 Peter was not reliable due to its authorial authenticity. He chose a different line of argumentation that intended to cut even deeper than a disagreement of the identity of the author behind the letter. He implied that it was pseudepigraphal and did not belong in the canon due to its lack of christological content. Interestingly, as this book has demonstrated, Käsemann's entire assumed premise and his christological conclusions were unfounded and misinformed.[6]

As stated in the first chapter, much of the research done in 2 Peter focused on Peter's eschatology. When one takes a step back and examines 2 Peter from a christological lens, not specifically focusing first on Peter's eschatology, a clear and rich picture emerges. The clarity of the picture causes one to wonder how Käsemann read the letter and was able to make such a comment that it is devoid of christological orientation. J. H. Neyrey, who in spite of his popular view of 2 Peter as pseudepigrapha, also challenged Käsemann's understanding of the lack of Christology in 2 Peter, writing, "[his views] are misplaced because his analysis did not attempt to understand 2 Peter in its proper historical context."[7] M. J. Kruger also concisely refuted Käsemann. He wrote:

> Käsemann and others also attack the Christology of the epistle and consider it to be deficient. He claims that the 'manward-oriented eschatology' pushes the lordship and prominence of Christ into the background. However, upon examination, the Christology of 2 Peter is an exalted one and consistent with the rest of the New Testament. The transfiguration of 1:17 declares Christ to be God's own son by the lips of the Father himself thus ensuring that power, majesty, honor and glory are his (1:16–17). Christ is given the titles of κύριος (14 times), σωτήρ (5 times)

---

5 Käsemann, "Apologia," 178.
6 Käsemann, "Apologia," 195.
7 Neyrey, "Form and Background," 407.

Conclusion

and δεσπότης (once), which all clearly emphasize his divinity and power. He is the one whose εντολή we must heed (2:21), it is only by him that we can hope to produce godly fruit (1:8), and it is by him that men find salvation (2:20). The doxology sums up the author's emphasis on Christ, 'Grow in the grace and knowledge of our Lord and Savior Jesus Christ. To him be glory both now and forever! Amen' (3:18).[8]

The conclusions of this book spoke in stark contrast to Käsemann's conclusions.

First, this work concluded that 2 Peter has a high Christology specifically in terms of Jesus' deity. Peter explicitly expressed Jesus' divinity employing four titles, θεός (God), κύριος (Lord), σωτήρ (Savior), and χριστός (Christ). He affirmed Jesus' divinity by denoting two of his divine attributes, his power and his divine nature. Peter also indirectly referenced Jesus' divinity when he spoke of him as Glory and Master Redeemer. Duane F. Watson and Terrance Callan affirmed this, writing, "Jesus Christ is God but distinct from God, and there is only one God. This view is reflected in every section of the letter except 2:10b–22. The Christology of 2 Peter is one of the most exalted in the New Testament."[9]

While Peter expressed his Christology in his own style and vocabulary, his presentation in 2 Peter is consistent with other New Testament presentations. Peter presented Jesus as the same God of the Old Testament, though often he referred to the Father when describing Old Testament events. For Peter, Jesus is also the promised Messiah, and that was not a logical problem for him to view Jesus as the Messiah and yet as divine. He portrayed Jesus as one who controls absolutely, yet with sacrifice, having given his own life for the redemption of mankind. Peter believed Jesus fully shares and embodies the glory of the Father. According to Peter, Jesus has equal power with God, since he is God and is of the same essence.

Second, the author of this work concluded that Peter also presented Jesus as unique and distinct from the Father. Peter presented Jesus as fully divine, yet as God the Son in relationship to God the Father, while holding to a monotheistic understanding. In Peter's monotheism, he spoke of Jesus as distinct from the Father. The Father exercises certain roles the Son does not, and vice versa. Peter also showed the Son to be unique. No one can compare Jesus to other sons of God. Jesus holds a special position as God. Jesus was the Son, by inference in 2 Peter, of God the Father due to his miraculous birth, and conception by the Holy Spirit. In demonstrating the

---

8 Kruger, "Authenticity of 2 Peter," 667.
9 Watson and Callan, *First and Second Peter*, 219.

unique distinctness of the Son from the Father, Peter presented the Father in three broad categories, as Preeminent Author, Magistrate, and Deliverer.

While Paul also called Jesus preeminent, Peter demonstrated the specific roles the Father played as Preeminent Author. Peter presented the Father as having a special role in creation. He also presented the Father as the Ruler of Time. Peter also highlighted the Father's role in inspiration as the Mover of Men, in concert with the Holy Spirit. As Magistrate, Peter identified the Father as Condemner of the unrighteous and unrighteousness and as Judge of all of his creation. Peter also underscored the Father's specific role as Deliverer, specifically as Patient Promise-Keeper, as Savior, and as Preserver of all of the righteous in Christ and according to his divine sovereignty.

The author of 2 Peter believed Jesus is the unique Son of God and is distinct from God the Father, even though both are fully God, along with the Holy Spirit, yet there is only one God. This book displayed specific events in Peter's life that would have shaped his understanding of the doctrine of the Godhead. Ron Adams spoke to the unity of 2 Peter with the New Testament and the ideas found within it, writing, "[The language] is found elsewhere in the New Testament: self-emptying language, self-denying language, language of endurance and perseverance in the face of persecution and hardship. We can at least hear Peter's words for what they appear to be: sincere counsel to those seeking to emulate the way of Jesus."[10] One sees a unified picture throughout the pages of the New Testament both in passages involving Peter and those written about him.

Lastly, the letter's doxology provided evidence that Peter held a high Christology and that it was consistent with his community and understanding. Richard J. Bauckham argued first that this was fitting for the time period in which Peter likely composed the epistle, writing, "Although doxologies to Christ are rare in early Christian literature, there is at least one unquestionable example from the first century (Rev 1:5–6), and so there is no need to date 2 Peter's in the second century."[11] Bauckham also noted that Peter's use of such a doxology was likely not a later addition, since "Their occasional appearance is in line with other evidence of a Christian attitude of worship toward Christ, which corresponded to his function in early Christianity."[12] The doxology fit Peter's context. For it was Peter's Christology that led him to his clear eschatological conclusions. Kruger commented, "We see that 2 Peter's eschatology—and his Christology and soteriology—is surprisingly

---

10 Adams, "Living by the Word," 23.
11 Bauckham, *Jude, 2 Peter*, 338.
12 Bauckham, *Jude, 2 Peter*, 338.

consistent with that of the NT. We can agree with Michael Green when he says, 'It would appear that these discrepancies in doctrine between 1 and 2 Peter are more fancied than real.'"[13] In fact, the readers of 2 Peter did not separate his Christology from eschatology. The goal of Peter's eschatology was Christ. John P. Meier added:

> The Christ who revealed himself of old to the apostles on the mount of transfiguration, the Christ who accurately predicted the death of Peter the Apostle in the first generation of the church, the Christ who even now shows patience and forbearance to sinners in the contemporary church, the Christ who will come in glory to bring both church and creation to their appointed goal, this Christ is, for 2 Peter, both the ground of stability and the principle of growth.[14]

Käsemann first looked into the eschatological arguments of 2 Peter and claimed he was not able to find any christological orientation. As the author of this work proposed, one must not look through eschatology to see the rich Christology that fills the verses of 2 Peter. However, when one first examines the christological language and themes within 2 Peter, one is faced with a beautiful portrayal of Jesus.

Peter's personal, spiritual, and reverent portrayal of Jesus causes one to be faced with Christ's divine beauty and glory. After truly experiencing the glory of Christ in the text of 2 Peter, one returns to eschatology, since the glory of Christ, as Peter portrayed him, draws the faithful to live abundant lives in the present characterized by the gospel, yet always looking forward to Jesus' imminent return, rule, and reign. Just as Peter's portrayal of Christ caused his readers to look to Christ in the present and in the future, so too do his words speak to all believers today.

---

13 Kruger, "Authenticity of 2 Peter," 669.
14 Meier, "Forming the Canon," 70.

Bibliography

Abbot, Edwin. "On the Second Epistle of St. Peter: I. Had the Author Read Josephus?" *Expositor* 2 (1882) 49–63.
Achtemeier, Paul J. *First Peter*. Hermenia Commentary Series. Minneapolis: Fortress, 1966.
———. "Suffering Servant and Suffering Christ in 1 Peter." In *The Future of Christology: Essays in Honor of Leander E. Keck*, edited by A. J. Malherbe and W. A. Meeks, 176–88. Minneapolis: Fortress, 1993.
———. "The Christology of 1 Peter: Some Reflections." In *Who Do You Say That I Am?: Essays on Christology*, edited by Mark Allan Powell and David Bauer, 140–54. Louisville: Westminster John Knox, 1999.
Adams, Edward. "Creation 'out of' and 'through' Water in 2 Peter 3:5." In *Creation of Heaven and Earth: Re-Interpretations of Genesis 1 in the Context of Judaism, Ancient Philosophy, Christianity, and Modern Physics*, edited by George H. van Kooten, 195–210. Leiden: Brill, 2005.
———. "The 'Coming of God' Tradition and Its Influence on New Testament Parousia Texts." In *Biblical Traditions in Transmission: Essays in Honor of Michael A. Knibb*, edited by Charlotte Hempel and Judith Lieu, 1–19. Leiden: Brill, 2006.
Adams, Ron. "Living by the Word." *Christian Century* 128:9 (2011) 22–23.
Aland, Barbara, Kurt Aland, and Bruce Metzger. *Novum Testamentum: Graece et Latine*. 27th ed. Münster: Deutsche Bibelgesellschaft, 2005.
Aland, Kurt. "Der Tod des Petrus in Rom." In *Kirchengeschichtliche Entwürfe: Alte Kirche, Reformation und Luthertum, Pietismus und Erweckungsbewegung*. Gütersloh: Mohn, 1960.
Aland, Kurt, Matthew Black, and Bruce Metzger. *The Greek New Testament*. 4th ed. Münster: United Bible Societies, 2007.
Alford, Henry. *Alford's Greek New Testament: An Exegetical and Critical Commentary*. 4 vols. Baker, 1980. Reprint, Franklin, TN: E-Sword 10.0.5, 2011.
Anatolios, Khaled. "Athanasius' Christology Today: The Life, Death, and Resurrection of Christ in *On the Incarnation*." In *The Shadow of the Incarnation*, edited by P. Martens, 29–49. Notre Dame, IN: Notre Dame University Press, 2008.
Archer, Gleason L. *Encyclopedia of Bible Difficulties*. Grand Rapids: Zondervan, 1982.
Armstrong, John H. "The Person of Christ." *Reformation & Revival* 8:4 (1999) 7–174.
Auer, Johann. "Die Bedeutung der Verklärung Christi für das Leben des Christen und für die Kirche Christi." In *Mysterien des Lebens Jesu und die christliche Existenz*, edited by Leo Scheffczyk, 146–76. Aschaffenburg, Germany: Paul Pattloch, 1984.

Aune, David E., ed. *The Westminster Dictionary of New Testament and Early Christian Literature and Rhetoric*. Louisville: Westminster John Knox, 2003.

Austinchael R. "Salvation and the Divinity of Jesus." *Expository Times* 96:9 (1985) 271–75.

Balz, Horst, and Wolfgang Shrage. *Die Katholischen Briefe*. Göttingen: Vandenhoeck and Ruprecht, 1973.

Barclay, William. *The Letters of James and Peter*. Daily Study Bible Series. Toronto: G. R. Welch, 1976.

Barker, Glenn W., William L. Lane, and J. Ramsey Michaels. *The New Testament Speaks*. New York: Harper & Row, 1969.

Barnes, Timothy. *Early Christian Hagiography and Roman History*. Tübingen: Mohr Siebeck, 2010.

Barnett, Albert E. *Paul Becomes a Literary Influence*. Chicago: University of Chicago Press, 1941.

Barry, John D. *Faithlife Study Bible*. Logos 4, Scholar's Library, Silver Edition. Bellingham, WA: Logos, 2016.

Bauckham, Richard J. "The Apocalypse of Peter: A Jewish Christian Apocalypse from the Time of Bar Kokhba." *Apocrypha* 5 (1994) 7–111.

———. "James, 1 and 2 Peter, Jude." In *It Is Written: Scripture Citing Scripture: Essays in Honour of Barnabas Lindars*, edited by D. A. Carson and H. G. M. Williamson, 303–17. Cambridge: Cambridge University Press, 1988.

———. *Jude, 2 Peter*. Word Biblical Commentary 50. Waco, TX: Word, 1983.

———. *Jude, 2 Peter*. In *Word Biblical Themes*. Dallas: Word, 1990.

———. "The Martyrdom of Peter in Early Christian Literature." In *Aufstieg und Niedergang der römischen Welt: Geschichte und Kultur Roms im Spiegel der neuren Forschung*, edited by H. Temporini and W. Haase: Principat 26.1, 539–95. Berlin: de Gruyter, 1992.

———. "2 Peter: An Account of Research." In *Aufstieg und Niedergang der römischen Welt: Geschichte und Kultur Roms im Spiegel der neuren Forschung*, edited by H. Temporini and W. Haase, Prinzipat 25.2, 3713–52. Berlin: de Gruyter, 1988.

———. "2 Peter and the Apocalypse of Peter." In *The Fate of the Dead: Studies on the Jewish and Christian Apocalypses*, 261–81. Leiden: Brill, 1998.

———. "2 Peter: A Supplementary Bibliography." *Journal of the Evangelical Theological Society* 25 (1982) 91–93.

———. "Pseudo-Apostolic Letters." *Journal of Biblical Literature* 107 (1988) 469–94.

Bauer, Walter. *A Greek-English Lexicon of the New Testament and Other Early Christian Literature*. 2nd ed. Translated by William F. Arndt, F. Wilbur Gingrich, and Frederick W. Danker. Chicago: University of Chicago Press, 1979.

Becker, Jürgen. "Ich bin die Auferstehung und das Leben: Eine Skizze der johanneischen Christologie." *Theologische Zeitschrift* 39:3 (1983) 138–51.

———. *Simon Petrus im Urchristentum*. Biblische-theologische Studien 105. Neukirchen-Vluyn, Germany: Neukirchener, 2009.

Beker, J. C. "Peter, Second Letter of." Vol. 3 in *Interpreter's Dictionary of the Bible*, edited by George Arthur Buttrick and John Knox, 767–69. Nashville: Abingdon, 1962.

Bénétreau, Samuel. "Évangile et prophétie: un texte original (1 P 1,10–12) peut-il éclairer un texte difficile (2 P 1,16–21)?" *Biblica* 86:2 (2005) 174–91.

Berger, Klaus. "Streit um Gottes Vorsehung. Zur Position der Gegner im 2. Petrusbrief." In *Tradition and Re-Interpretation in Jewish and Christian Literature: Essays in*

Honour of Jürgen C. H. Lebram, edited by J. W. van Henten, H. J. De Jonge, P. T. van Rooden, and W. Wesselius, 121–35. Leiden: Brill, 1986.

Betz, Otto. "Die Bileamtradition und die biblische Lehre von der Inspiration." In *Religion im Erbe Ägyptens: Beiträge zur spätantiken Religionsgeschichte zu Ehren von Alexander Böhlig*, edited by Manfred Görg, 18–53. Wiesbaden, Germany: Otto Harrassowitz, 1988.

Bigg, Charles. *A Critical and Exegetical Commentary on the Epistles of St. Peter and St. Jude.* International Critical Commentary. New York: Scribner, 1901.

Billings, Bradly S. "'The Angels Who Sinned . . . He Cast into Tartarus' (2 Peter 2:4): Its Ancient Meaning and Present Relevance." *Expository Times* 119:11 (2008) 532–37.

Black, David Alan, and David S. Dockery, eds. *Interpreting the New Testament: Essays on Methods and Issues.* Nashville: Broadman & Holman, 2001.

Blair, Joe. *Introducing the New Testament.* Nashville: Broadman & Holman, 1994.

Blumenthal, Christian. "'Göttliche Natur' versus 'grosse Art': Theologie und Chrsitologie in der fayumischen Übersetzung von 2Petr in P.Mich. 3520." *Zeitschrift für die neutestamentliche Wissenschaft und die Kunde der älteren Kirche* 103:2 (2012) 272–82.

———. "Hoffnung für die Gegner? zur fayumischen Übersetzung von 2Petr 3 in P.Mich. 3520 und zugleich ein Beitrag zur Rezeptionsgeschichte dieses Briefes." *Zeitschrift für die neutestamentliche Wissenschaft und die Kunde der älteren Kirche* 103:1 (2012) 111–35.

Bockmuehl, Markus. *Seeing the Word: Refocusing New Testament Study.* Studies in Theological Interpretation. Grand Rapids: Baker, 2006.

———. *Simon Peter in Scripture and Memory: The New Testament Apostle in the Early Church.* Grand Rapids: Baker, 2012.

Boobyer, G. H. "The Indebtedness of 2 Peter to 1 Peter." In *New Testament Essays: Studies in Memory of Thomas Walter Manson*, edited by A. J. B. Higgins, 34–53. Manchester: Manchester University Press, 1959.

Boring, M. Eugene, Klaus Berger, and Carsten Colpe, eds. *Hellenistic Commentary to the New Testament.* Nashville: Abingdon, 1995.

Bouchât, Robert Alan. "Dating the Second Epistle of Peter." PhD diss,. Baylor University, 1992.

Boyd, Gregory. *Across the Spectrum: Understanding Issues in Evangelical Theology.* Grand Rapids: Baker, 2009.

Boyer, James L. "Relative Clauses in the Greek New Testament: A Statistical Study." *Grace Theological Journal* 9 (1988) 233–56.

Brannan, Rich. *The Lexham Analytical Lexicon to the Greek New Testament.* Logos 4, Scholars Library, Silver Edition. Bellingham, WA: Logos, 2011.

Bratcher, Robert G. *A Translator's Guide to the Letters of James, Peter, and Jude.* New York: United Bible Societies, 1984.

Brown, Raymond E. *An Introduction to New Testament Christology.* New York: Paulist, 1994.

Brown, Raymond E., Karl P. Donfried, and John Reumann, eds. *Peter in the New Testament: A Collaborative Assessment by Protestant and Roman Catholic Scholars.* Minneapolis: Paulist, 1973.

Brown, Raymond E., and John P. Meier. *Antioch and Rome: New Testament Cradles of Catholic Christianity.* New York: Paulist, 1983.

Bruce, F. F., ed. *The International Bible Commentary.* Grand Rapids: Zondervan, 1986.

Buis, Harry. "The Significance of II Timothy 3:16 and II Peter 1:21." *Reformed Review* 14:3 (1961) 43–49.

Burge, Gary, Lynn Cohick, and Gene Green. *The New Testament in Antiquity*. Grand Rapids: Zondervan, 2009.

Busch, Austin. "Presence Deferred: The Name of Jesus and Self-Referential Eschatological Prophecy in Acts 3." *Biblical Interpretation* 17:5 (2009) 521–53.

Callan, Terrance. "The Christology of the Second Letter of Peter." *Biblica* 82:2 (2001) 253–63.

———. "Comparison of Humans to Animals in 2 Peter 2,10b–22." *Biblica* 90:1 (2009) 101–13.

———. *Dying and Rising with Christ: The Theology of Paul the Apostle*. New York: Paulist, 2006.

———. "A Note on 2 Peter 1:1–7." *Journal of Biblical Literature* 125 (2006) 143–50.

———. *The Origins of Christian Faith*. New York: Paulist, 1994.

———. "The Soteriology of the Second Letter of Peter." *Biblica* 82 (2001) 549–59.

———. "The Style of the Second Letter of Peter." *Biblica* 84 (2003) 202–24.

———. "The Syntax of 2 Peter 1:1–7." *Catholic Biblical Quarterly* 67:4 (2005) 632–40.

———. "The Use of the Letter of Jude by the Second Letter of Peter." *Biblica* 85 (2004) 42–64.

Carder, Muriel M. "An Enquiry into the Textual Transmission of Catholic Epistles," PhD diss., Victoria University, 1968.

Carson, D. A., Douglas J. Moo, and Leon Morris. *An Introduction to the New Testament*. Grand Rapids: Zondervan, 1992.

Carson, D. A., R. T. France, J. A. Motyer, and G. J. Wenham, eds. *New Bible Commentary*. Downer's Grove, IL: InterVarsity, 1994.

Cate, James Jeffrey. "The Text of the Catholic Epistles and the Revelation in the Writings of Origen," PhD diss., New Orleans Baptist Theological Seminary, 1997.

Caulley, Thomas S. "The False Teachers in Second Peter." *Studia Biblica et Theologica* 12 (1982) 27–42.

———. "The Idea of Inspiration in 2 Peter 1:16–21." PhD diss., Universität Tübingen, 1983.

Cavallin, H. C. C. "The False Teachers of 2 Peter as Pseudoprophets." *Novum Testamentum* 21 (1979) 263–70.

Cedar, Paul A. *James, 1, 2 Peter, Jude*. Communicator's Commentary 11. Waco, TX: Word, 1984.

Chang, A. D. "Second Peter 2:1 and the Extent of the Atonement." *Bibliotheca Sacra* 142 (1985) 522–63.

Charles, J. Daryl. "The Language and Logic of Virtue in 2 Peter 1:5–7." *Bulletin for Biblical Research* 8 (1998) 55–73.

Charles, J. Daryl. *Virtue amidst Vice: The Catalog of Virtues in 2 Peter 1*. Journal for the Study of the New Testament Supplement Series 150. Sheffield, England: Sheffield, 1997.

Chester, Andrew, and Ralph P. Martin. *The Theology of the Letters of James, Peter, and Jude*. New Testament Theology. Cambridge: Cambridge University Press, 1994.

Childs, Brevard S. *The New Testament as Canon*. Philadelphia: Fortress, 1984.

Chilton, Bruce, and Craig Evans, eds. *The Missions of James, Peter, and Paul*. Leiden: Brill, 2005.

Clinton, Stephen M. "Conceptual Foundations for Theosis and Postmodern Theology." *American Theological Inquiry* 2:2 (2009) 61–66.

Corley, Bruce, Steve W. Lemke, and Grant I. Lovejoy, eds. *Biblical Hermeneutics: A Comprehensive Introduction to Interpreting Scriptures.* Nashville: Broadman & Holman, 2002.

Couch, Mal, ed. *An Introduction to Classical Evangelical Hermeneutics: A Guide to the History and Practice of Biblical Interpretation.* Grand Rapids: Kregel, 2000.

Craddock, Fred B., Jr. *First and Second Peter and Jude.* Westminster Bible Companion. Louisville: Westminster John Knox, 1995.

Crehan, J. "New Light on 2 Peter from the Bodmer Papyrus." *Studia Evangelica* 7 (1982) 145–49.

Crowe, Brandon D. *The Message of the General Epistles in the History of Redemption.* Phillipsburg, NJ: P&R, 2015.

Cruz, Roli G de la. "Luke's Application of Joel 2:28–32 in Peter's Sermon in Acts 2." *Cyberjournal for Pentecostal-Charismatic Research* 4, (1998). ATLA Religion Database.

Cullman, Oscar. *The Christology of the New Testament.* Translated by S. C. Guthrie and C. A. M. Hall. Philadelphia: Westminster, 1959.

Dalton, William. "The Interpretation of 1 Peter 3:19 and 4:6: Light from 2 Peter." *Biblia* 60 (1979) 547–55.

Danker, Frederick W. *Benefactor: Epigraphic Study of a Graeco-Roman and New Testament Semantic Field.* St. Louis: Clayton, 1982.

———. "II Peter 3:10 and Psalm of Solomon 17:10." *Zeitschrift für die neutestamentliche Wissenschaft* 53 (1962) 82–86.

———. "2 Peter 1: A Solemn Decree." *Catholic Biblical Quarterly* 40 (1978) 64–82.

Davids, Peter H. *The Letters of 2 Peter and Jude.* Pillar New Testament Commentary. Grand Rapids: Eerdmans, 2006.

———. "The Pseudepigrapha in the Catholic Epistles." In *The Pseudepigrapha and Early Biblical Interpretation*, edited by James H. Charlesworth and Craig A. Evans, 228–245. Journal for the Study of the Pseudepigrapha, Supplement Series 14. Sheffield: Journal for the Study of the Old Testament Press, 1993.

———. *A Theology of James, Peter, and Jude.* Grand Rapids: Zondervan, 2014.

Davies, Paul E. "Primitive Christology in 1 Peter." In *Festschrift to Honor F. Wilbur Gingrich*, edited by Eugene H. Barth and Ronald E. Cocroft, 115–22. Leiden: Brill, 1972.

De Jonge, Marinus. *Christology in Context: The Earliest Christian Response to Jesus.* Philadelphia: Westminster, 1988.

Desjardins, M. "The Portrayal of the Dissidents in 2 Peter and Jude: Does It Tell Us More about the 'Godly' than the 'Ungodly'?" *Journal for the Study of the New Testament* 30 (1987) 89–102.

Dockery, David S., Trent C. Butler, Christopher L. Church, eds. *Holman Bible Handbook.* Nashville: Holman, 1992.

Donaldson, T. "Parallels: Uses and Limitations. *Evangelical Quarterly* 55 (1983) 193–210.

Donelson, Lewis R. *1 and 2 Peter and Jude: A Commentary.* New Testament Library. Louisville: Westminster John Knox, 2010.

Dowd, Sharyn. "2 Peter." In *The Women's Bible Commentary*, edited by Carol A. Newsom and Sharon H. Ringe, 373. Louisville: Westminster John Knox, 1992.

Dschulnigg, Peter. "Der theologische Ort des Zweiten Petrusbriefs." *Biblische Zeitschrift* 33 (1989) 161–77.

Dubis, Mark. "First Peter and the Sufferings of the Messiah." In *Looking into the Future: Evangelical Studies in Eschatology*, edited by David Baker, 85–96. Grand Rapids: Baker Academic, 2001.

Duke, Thomas H. "An Exegetical Analysis of 2 Peter 3:9." *Faith and Mission* 16:3 (1999) 6–13.

Dunham, D. A. "An Exegetical Study of 2 Peter 2:18–22." *Bibliotheca Sacra* 140 (1983) 40–54.

Dunn, James D. G. *Unity and Diversity in the New Testament: An Enquiry into the Character of Earliest Christianity*. London: SCM, 1990.

Dunn, James D. G., and John W. Rogerson, eds. *Eerdmans Commentary on the Bible*. Grand Rapids: Eerdmans, 2003.

Dunnet, W. M. "The Hermeneutics of Jude and 2 Peter: The Use of Ancient Jewish Traditions." *Journal of the Evangelical Theological Society* 31 (1988) 287–92.

Du Toit, Marietjie. "The Expression Logikon Adolon Gala as the Key to 1 Peter 2:1–3." *Hervormde Teologiese Studies* 63:1 (2007) 221–29.

Easton, M. *Easton's Bible Dictionary*. 1897. Logos 4, Scholars Library, Silver Edition. Oak Harbor, WA: Logos, 1996.

Ebright, Homer Kingsley. *The Petrine Epistles: A Critical Study of Authorship*. Cincinnati: Methodist Book Concern, 1917.

Ehrman, Bart. *The New Testament: A Historical Introduction to the Early Christian Writings*. New York: Oxford University Press, 1997.

———. *The Orthodox Corruption of Scripture: The Effect of Early Christological Controversies on the Text of the New Testament*. New York: Oxford University Press, 1993.

Elliott, John H. *James, 1 and 2 Peter, Jude*. Augsburg Commentary on the New Testament.. Minneapolis: Augsburg, 1982.

———. "A Catholic Gospel: Reflections on 'Early Catholicism' in the New Testament." *Catholic Biblical Quarterly* 31 (1969) 213–23.

———. "Peter, Second Epistle of." In *Anchor Bible Dictionary*, edited by David Noel Friedman, 5:282–87. New York: Doubleday, 1992.

———. "Peter, Silvanus and Mark in 1 Peter and Acts: Sociological-Exegetical Perspectives on a Petrine Group in Rome." In *Wort in der Zeit: Neutestamentliche Studien: K. H. Rengstorf Festschrift*, edited by W. Haubeck and M. Bachmann, 250–67. Leiden: Brill, 1980.

Ellis, Earle E. "Pseudonymity and Canonicity of New Testament Documents." In *Worship, Theology and Ministry in the Early Church: Essays in Honor of Ralph P. Martin*, edited by Michael J. Wilkins and Terence Paige, 212–24. Journal for the Study of the New Testament, Supplement Series 87. Sheffield: Journal for the Study of the Old Testament Press, 1992.

Elwell, Walter A., ed. *Evangelical Commentary on the Bible*. Grand Rapids: Baker, 1986.

———, ed. *Evangelical Dictionary of Biblical Theology*. Grand Rapids: Baker, 1996.

———, ed. *Evangelical Dictionary of Theology*. Grand Rapids: Baker, 1984.

Enns, Paul P. *The Moody Handbook of Theology*. Chicago: Moody, 1989.

Erbes, Carl. "Petrus nicht in Rom, sondern in Jerusalem gestorben." *Zeitschrift für Kirchengeschichte* 22 (1901) 1–47, 161–231.

Evans, Craig A., Robert L. Webb, and Richard A. Wiebe, eds. *Nag Hammadi Texts and the Bible*. Leiden: Brill, 1993.

Falconer, R. "Is 2 Peter a Genuine Epistle to the Christians of Samaria?" *Expositor* 6:5 (1902) 459–72; 6:6 (1902) 47–56, 117–27, 218–27.

Farkasfalvy, Denis. "The Ecclesial Setting and Pseudepigraphy in 2 Peter and Its Role in the Formation of the Canon." *Second Century: A Journal of Early Christian Studies* 5:1 (1986) 3–29.

Farmer, Donald. "The Lord's Supper until He Comes." *Grace Theological Journal* 6 (1985) 391–401.

Farmer, William R. "Some Critical Reflections on 2 Peter: A Response to a Paper on 2 Peter by Denis Farkasfalvy." *Second Century: A Journal of Early Christian Studies* 5 (1985) 30–46.

Farrar, F. "Dr. Abbott on the Second Epistle of St. Peter and Josephus." *Expositor* 3 (1888) 58–69.

Felix, Paul W. "Penal Substitution in the New Testament: A Focused Look at First Peter." *Master's Seminary Journal* 20:2 (2009) 171–97.

Ferguson, Everett. *Backgrounds of Early Christianity*. Grand Rapids: Eerdmans, 1993.

Ferguson, Sinclair B., and David F. Wright, eds. *New Dictionary of Theology*. Downers Grove, IL: InterVarsity, 1988.

Fornberg, T. *An Early Church in a Pluralistic Society: A Study of 2 Peter*. Coniectanea Biblica, New Testament Series 9. Lund, England: Gleerup, 1977.

Fry, Evan. "Commentaries on James, 1 and 2 Peter, and Jude." *Bible Today* 41 (1990) 326–36.

Gaebelein, Frank E., ed. *The Expositor's Bible Commentary*, vol. 12. Grand Rapids: Zondervan, 1981.

Garnet, Paul. "O'Callaghan's Fragments: Our Earliest New Testament Texts?" *Evangelical Quarterly* 45 (1973) 6–12.

Gempf, Conrad. "Pseudonymity and the New Testament." *Themelios* 17 (1992) 8–10.

Gilmourchael, J. "How to Approach a Strange Manuscript: A Novel('s) Look at the Historical Task." *Arc* 27 (1999) 97–107.

———. "Reflections on the Authorship of 2 Peter." *Evangelical Quarterly* 73 (2001) 107–22.

———. "The Significance of Parallels between 2 Peter and Other Early Christian Literature," PhD diss., McGill University, 2012.

———. "2 Peter in Recent Research: A Bibliography." *Journal of the Evangelical Society* 42 (1999) 673–78.

Green, G. L. "'As for Prophecies, They Will Come to an End': 2 Peter, Paul and Plutarch on 'the Obsolescence of Oracles.'" *Journal for the Study of the New Testament* 82 (2001) 107–22.

Green, Michael. *The Second Epistle General of Peter and the General Epistle of Jude*. Tyndale New Testament Commentary. Grand Rapids: Eerdmans, 1988.

———. *2 Peter Reconsidered*. London, England: Tyndale, 1960.

Gruenler, Royce Gordon. *New Approaches to Jesus and the Gospels: A Phenomenological and Exegetical Study of Synoptic Christology*. Grand Rapids: Baker, 1982.

Gundry, Robert Horton. *A Survey of the New Testament*. Grand Rapids: Zondervan, 1970.

Guthrie, Donald. *New Testament Introduction*. Downers Grove, IL: InterVarsity, 1970.

Hafemann, Scott J. "Salvation in Jude 5 and the Argument of 2 Peter 1:3–11." In *Catholic Epistles and Apostolic Tradition*, edited by Karl-Wilhelm Niebuhr and Robert W. Wall, 331–42. Waco, TX: Baylor, 2009.

Hall, Stuart G. "Synoptic Transfigurations: Mark 9:2–10 and Partners." *King's Theological Review* 10:2 (1987) 41–44.

Harnik, Douglas. *First and Second Peter*. Brazos Theological Commentary on the Bible. Grand Rapids: Brazos, 2009.

Harrington, Daniel J. *First Peter, Jude, and Second Peter*. Sacra Pagina. Collegeville, MN: Liturgical, 2003.

Harrison, Everett Falconer. *An Introduction to the New Testament*. Grand Rapids: Eerdmans, 1971.

Harris, W. Wall, ed. *The NET Bible First Edition Notes*. Logos 4, Scholars Library, Silver Edition. Bellingham, WA: Logos, 2016.

Harvey, A. E. "The Testament of Simeon Peter." In *A Tribute to Geza Vermes: Essays on Jewish and Christian Literature and History*, edited by Philip R. Davies and Richard T. White, 339–54. Journal for the Study of the Old Testament, Supplement Series 100. Sheffield: Journal for the Study of the Old Testament Press, 1990.

Head, Peter M. "On the Christology of the Gospel of Peter." *Vigiliae Christianae* 46:3 (1992) 209–24.

Heever, G. van der. "In Purifying Fire: World View and 2 Peter 3:10." *Neotestamentica* 27 (1993) 107–18.

Heide, G. Z. "What Is New about the New Heaven and the New Earth? A Theology of Creation from Revelation 21 and 2 Peter 3." *Journal of the Evangelical Theological Society* 40 (1997) 37–56.

Heiserchael, S., and Vincent M. Setterholm. *Glossary of Morpho-Syntactic Database Terminology*. Logos 4, Scholars Library, Silver Edition. Bellingham, WA: Logos, 2013.

Helm, David. *First and Second Peter and Jude: Sharing Christ's Sufferings*. Preaching the Word. Wheaton, IL: Crossway, 2008.

Helyer, Larry. *The Life and Witness of Peter*. Downers Grove, IL: InterVarsity, 2012.

Hiebert, D. Edmond. *Second Peter and Jude*. Greenville, SC: Unusual Publications, 1989.

———. "Selected Studies from 2 Peter. Part 1: The Necessary Growth in the Christian Life: An Exposition of 2 Peter 1:5–11." *Bibliotheca Sacra* 141 (1984) 43–54.

———. "Selected Studies from 2 Peter. Part 2: The Prophetic Foundation for the Christian Life: An Exposition of 2 Peter 1:19–21." *Bibliotheca Sacra* 141 (1984) 158–68.

———. "Selected Studies from 2 Peter. Part 3: A Portrayal of False Teachers: An Exposition of 2 Peter 2:1–3." *Bibliotheca Sacra* 141 (1984) 255–65.

———. "Selected Studies from 2 Peter. Part 4: Directives for Living in Dangerous Days: An Exposition of 2 Peter 3:14–18a." *Bibliotheca Sacra* 141 (1984) 330–40.

Hillyer, Norman. *1 and 2 Peter, Jude*. New International Biblical Commentary 16. Peabody, MA: Hendrickson, 1992.

Himes, Paul A. "Peter and the Prophetic Word: The Theology of Prophecy Traced through Peter's Sermons and Epistles." *Bulletin for Biblical Research* 21:2 (2011) 227–43.

Hughes, Robert B., and J. Carl Laney, eds. *Tyndale Concise Bible Commentary*. Wheaton, IL: Tyndale, 2001.

Hupper, W. "Additions to 'A 2 Peter Bibliography.'" *Journal of the Evangelical Theological Society* 23 (1980) 65–66.
Hutton, Rodney R. "Moses on the Mount of Transfiguration." *Hebrew Annual Review* 14 (1994) 99–120.
Jackson, Jeffrey Glen. *Jude–2 Peter Parallels*. Logos 4, Scholars Library, Silver Edition. Oak Harbor, WA: Logos, 2009.
Jacobs, Paul E. "Exegetical-Devotional Study of 2 Peter 1:16–21." *Springfielder* 28:2 (1964) 18–30.
Jamieson, Robert, and A. R. Fausset, et al. *A Commentary, Critical and Explanatory, on the Old and New Testaments*. 1871. Logos 4, Scholars Library, Silver Edition. Oak Harbor, WA: Logos, 1997.
Jens, Walter. *Theologie und Literatur: Möglichkeiten und Grenzen eines Dialogs im 20 Jahrhundert*. In *Theologie und Literatur*, 30–56. Munich: Kindler, 1986.
Kahmann, Johannes. "The Second Letter of Peter and the Letter of Jude: Their Mutual Relationship." In *The New Testament in Early Christianity: La Réception des ecrits Néotestamentaires dans le Christianisme Primitive*, edited by Jean-Marie Sevrin, 105–21. Leuven: Leuven University Press, 1989.
Käsemann, Ernst. "An Apologia for Primitive Christian Eschatology." In *Essays on New Testament Themes*, translated by W. J. Montague, 169–95. London: SCM, 1964.
Keener, Craig S. *The IVP Bible Background Commentary: New Testament*. Logos 4, Scholars Library, Silver Edition. Oak Harbor, WA: Logos, 1993.
Kennard, Douglas Welker. "Petrine Redemption: Its Meaning and Extent." *Journal of the Evangelical Theological Society* 30:4 (1987) 399–405.
Kilgallen, John J. "'With Many Other Words' (Acts 2,40): Theological Assumptions in Peter's Pentecost Speech." *Biblica* 83:1 (2002) 71–87.
King, Marcahnt. "Jude and 1 and 2 Peter: Notes on the Bodmer Manuscript." *Bibliotheca Sacra* 121 (1969) 54–57.
Kistemaker, Simon J. *Exposition of the Epistles of Peter and of the Epistle of Jude*. Grand Rapids: Baker, 1987.
Kittel, Gerhard and Gerhard Friedrich, eds. *Theological Dictionary of the New Testament*. Translated by Geoffrey William Bromiley. 10 vols. Grand Rapids: Eerdmans, 1995.
Klein, Dietrich. *Hermann Samuel Reimarus (1694–1768): Das theologische Werk*. Tübingen: Mohr, 2009.
Klinger, Jerzy. "The Second Epistle of Peter: An Essay in Understanding." Translated by Paul Garrett. *St. Vladimir's Theological Quarterly* 17 (1973) 152–69.
Knoch, Otto. "Gab es eine Petrusschule in Rom?" *Studien zum Neuen Testament und seiner Umwelt* A–16 (1991) 105–26.
Koger, A. Dennis, Jr. "The Question of a Distinctive Petrine Theology in the New Testament." PhD diss., Baylor University, 1988.
Kolp, Alan L. "Partakers of the Divine Nature: The Use of 2 Peter 1:4 by Athanasius." *Studia Patristica* 17 (1982) 1018–23.
Kraus, Thomas J. "Para kyriou, para kyriō oder omit in 2 Petr 2,11: Textkritik und Interpretation vor dem Hintergrund juristischer Diktion und der Verwendung von para." *Zeitschrift für die neutestamentliche Wissenschaft und die Kunde der älteren Kirche* 91:3–4 (2000) 265–73.
Kruger, M. J. "The Authenticity of 2 Peter." *Journal of the Evangelical Theological Society* 42 (1999) 645–71.
Kuhn, Karl A. "2 Peter 3:1–3." *Interpretation* 60:3 (2006) 310–12.

Kümmel, Werner G. *Introduction to the New Testament*. Translated by Howard Clark Kee. New York: Abingdon, 1975.

Kuske, David P. "Exegetical Brief: Conveyed from Heaven 2 Peter 1:17, 18, 21." *Wisconsin Lutheran Quarterly* 99:1 (2002) 55–57.

Lamberton, David. "New England Bible College External Studies Course B i 116, General Epistles (1–2 Peter, Jude, 1–3 John)." PhD diss., Western Conservative Baptist Theological Seminary, 1995.

Lapham, F. *Peter: The Myth, the Man, and the Writings*. London: Sheffield Academic, 2003.

Lauritsen, Dennis. "The Suffering Servants of 1 Peter." *Lutheran Forum* 43:2 (2009) 13–17.

Legasse, Simon. "Review of Klaus Berger: 'Theologiegeschichte des Urchristentums.'" *Biblia* 77 (1996) 278–81.

Lenhard, von Helmut. "Ein Beitrag zur Übersetzung von 2 Peter 3." *Zeitschrift für die neutestamentliche Wissenschaft* 52 (1961) 128–29.

Lias, J. "The Genuineness of the Second Epistle of St. Peter. *Bibliotheca Sacra* 70 (1913) 599–606.

Liddell, Henri George. *A Lexicon: Abridged from Liddell and Scott's Greek-English Lexicon*. Logos 4, Scholars Library, Silver Edition. Oak Harbor, WA: Logos, 1996.

Louw, Johannes P., and Eugene Albert Nida, eds. *Greek-English Lexicon of the New Testament: Based on Semantic Domains*. New York: United Bible Societies, 1996.

Lövestam, E. "Eschatologie und Tradition im 2. Petrusbrief." In *The New Testament Age: Essays in Honor of Bo Reicke*, edited by W. C. Weinrich, 287–300. Macon, GA: Mercer University, 1984.

Loh, I-Jin. "Who Does 'His' in 'His Divine Grace' Refer to in 2 Peter 1:3?" *Taiwan Journal of Theology* 23 (2001) 105–28.

Lucas, Dick, and Christopher Green. *The Message of 2 Peter and Jude*. Downers Grove, IL: InterVarsity, 1995.

Lukaszewski, Albert L. *The Lexham Syntactic Greek New Testament Glossary*. Logos 4, Scholars Library, Silver Edition. Bellingham, WA: Logos, 2007.

Lukaszewski, Albert L., and Mark Dubis. *The Lexham Syntactic Greek New Testament: Expansions and Annotations*. Logos 4, Scholars Library, Silver Edition. Bellingham, WA: Logos, 2009.

Makujina, John. "The 'Trouble' with Lot in 2 Peter: Locating Peter's Source for Lot's Torment." *Westminster Theological Journal* 60 (1998) 255–69.

Marcuson, Margaret J. "Focus: 2 Peter 3:8–15a: (Wait Patiently for the Day of the Lord)." *Clergy Journal* 84:7 (2008) 72–74.

Marshall, I. Howard. "Review of Richard J. Bauckham: 'Jude, 2 Peter.'" *Evangelical Quarterly* 57 (1985) 78.

Martin, Ralph P., and Peter Davids, eds. *Dictionary of the Later New Testament and Its Developments*. Downers Grove, IL: InterVarsity, 1997.

Martin, Raymond A. *Syntax Criticism of Johannine Literature, the Catholic Epistles, and the Gospel Passion Accounts*. Studies in Bible and Early Christianity 18. Lewiston, NY: Edwin Mellen, 1989.

Mayhue, Richard. "The Apostle's Watchword: Day of the Lord." In *New Testament Essays in Honor of Homer A. Kent, Jr*, edited by Gary T. Meadors, 239–63. Winona Lake, IN: BMH, 1991.

Mayor, J. B. *The Epistle of St. Jude and the Second Epistle of St. Peter*. London: Macmillan, 1907.

Mayr, Ernst. *Novum Testamentum: Graece et Latine*. 28th ed. Münster: Deutsche Bibelgesellschaft, 2013.
McNamara, M. "The Unity of Second Peter: A Reconsideration." *Studies in Comparative Religion* 12 (1960) 13–19.
Meade, David G. *Pseudonymity and Canon: An Investigation into the Relationship of Authorship and Authority in Jewish and Earliest Christian Tradition*. Wissenschaftliche Untersuchungen zur Neuen Testament 39. Tübingen: Mohr, 1986.
Meier, John P. "Forming the Canon on the Edge of the Canon: 2 Peter 3:8–18." *Mid-Stream* 38:1–2 (1999) 65–70.
Meier, Sam. "2 Peter 3:3–7—An Early Jewish and Christian Response to Eschatological Skepticism." *Biblische Zeitschrift* 32 (1988) 255–57.
Metzger, Bruce Manning. *A Textual Commentary on the Greek New Testament*. New York: United Bible Societies, 1994.
Michaels, J. Ramsey. *First Peter*. Word Biblical Commentary 49. Waco, TX: Word, 1988.
———. "Second Peter and Jude—Royal Promises." In *The New Testament Speaks*, edited by Glenn W. Barker, William L. Lane, and J. Ramsey Michaels, 346–61. New York: Harper & Row, 1969.
Miller, Charles Armand. "Peter's Pentecostal Sermon." *Lutheran Church Review* 22 (1903) 552–64.
Miller, Robert J. "Is There Independent Attestation for the Transfiguration in 2 Peter?" *New Testament Studies* 42:4 (1996) 620–25.
Moberly, R. W. L. "'Who Is Jesus Christ for Us Today?' Peter's Confession (Matthew 6.13–28) Reconsidered." In *Christology and Scripture*, edited by Andrew T. Lincoln and Angus Paddison, 7–21. London: T. & T. Clark, 2007.
Moo, Douglas J. *2 Peter, Jude*. New International Version Application Commentary. Grand Rapids: Zondervan, 1996.
Moore, Andrew. "Who Are the Liberals Now? History, Science, and Christology in N. T. Wright and Alister McGrath." *Anvil* 20:1 (2003) 9–24.
Morris, Ryan Dale. "Preaching Difficult Passages: An Exegetical and Homiletical Analysis of Difficulties in Selected Petrine Passages." PhD diss., Mid-America Baptist Theological Seminary, 2009.
Neufeld, K. "'Frühkatholizismus'—Idee und Begriff." *Zeitschrift für Theologie und Kirche* 94 (1972) 1–28.
Neyrey, J. H. "The Apologetic Use of the Transfiguration in 2 Peter 1:16–21." *Catholic Biblical Quarterly* 42 (1980) 504–19.
———. "The Form and Background of the Polemic in 2 Peter." *Journal of Biblical Literature* 99 (1980) 407–31.
———. *2 Peter, Jude*. Anchor Bible 37C. Garden City, NY: Doubleday, 1993.
———. "The Second Epistle of Peter." In *The New Jerome Biblical Commentary*, edited by Raymond E. Brown, Joseph A. Fitzmyer, and Roland E. Murphy, section 64, pp. 1017–22. Englewood Cliffs, NJ: Prentice-Hall, 1990.
Nicoll, W. *The Expositor's Greek New Testament*. 5 vols. Eerdmans, 1960. Reprint, Franklin, TN: E-Sword 10.0.5, 2011.
Nienhuis, David R., and Robert W. Wall. *Reading the Epistles of James, Peter, John, and Jude as Scripture*. Grand Rapids: Eerdmans, 2013.
O'Keefe, Mark. "Theosis and the Christian Life: Toward Integrating Roman Catholic Ethics and Spirituality." *Eglise et Théologie* 25 (1994) 47–63.

Ollerton, Andrew J. "Quasi Deificari: Deification in the Theology of John Calvin." *Westminster Theological Journal* 73:2 (2011) 237–54.

Overstreet, R. Larry. "A Study of 2 Peter 3:10–13." *Bibliotheca Sacra* 137 (1980) 354–71.

Packer, James I. "A Lamp in a Dark Place: 2 Peter 1:19–21." In *Can We Trust the Bible?: Leading Theologians Speak Out on Biblical Inerrancy*, edited by Earl D. Radmacher, 15–30. Wheaton, IL: Tyndale, 1979.

Pančovski, Ivan. "Tugend: Weg zum Heil." *Ostkirchliche Studien* 32:2–3 (1983) 105–16.

Panning, Armin J. "What Has Been Determined (etethēsan) in 1 Peter 2:8?" *Wisconsin Lutheran Quarterly* 98:1 (2001) 48–52.

Papias. "Fragments of Papias." In *The Apostolic Fathers with Justin Martyr and Irenaeus*, vol. 1 of *Ante-Nicene Fathers*. Edited by Alexander Roberts, James Donaldson, and A. Cleveland Coxe. Buffalo, NY: Christian Literature, 1885.

Paulsen, Henning. *Der Zweite Petrusbrief und der Judasbrief*. Kritisch-exegetischer Kommentar über das Neue Testament 12. Göttingen: Vandenhoeck & Ruprecht, 1992.

Pearson, Birger A. "The Apocalypse of Peter and Canonical 2 Peter." In *Gnosticism and the Early Christian World: In Honor of James M. Robinson*, edited by J. E. Goehring, C. W. Hedrick, J. T. Sanders, and H. D. Betz, 67–74. Sonoma, CA: Polebridge, 1990.

———. "James, 1–2 Peter, Jude." In *The New Testament and Its Modern Interpreters*, edited by Eldon Jay Epp and George W. MacRae, 371–406. Philadelphia: Fortress, 1989.

———. "A Reminiscence of Classical Myth at II Peter 2:4." *Greek, Roman and Byzantine Studies* 10:1 (1969) 71–80.

Perkins, Pheme. *First and Second Peter, James, and Jude*. Interpretation. Louisville: Harper, 1995.

———. *Peter: Apostle for the Whole Church*. Minneapolis: Fortress, 2009.

———. "Peter's Pentecost Sermon: A Limitation on Who May Minister." In *Women Priests: A Catholic Commentary on the Vatican Declaration*, edited by Arlene Swidler and Leonard Swidler, 156–58. New York: Paulist, 1977.

Pesch, Rudolph. *Die biblischen Grundlagen des Primats*. Freiburg: Herder, 2001.

Peterson, Robert A. "Apostasy." *Presbyterion* 19:1 (1993) 17–31.

Petrey, Taylor G. "Practicing Divinity." *Dialogue* 42:2 (2009) 179–82.

Picirilli, R. E. "Allusions to 2 Peter in the Apostolic Fathers." *Journal for the Study of the New Testament* 33 (1988) 57–83.

Pouncey, Gregory Thomas. "The Canonical History of 2 Peter in Light of Four Theological Issues of the Second Century." PhD diss., Southwestern Baptist Theological Seminary, 1995.

Powell, Mark Allan, and David R. Bauer, eds. *Who Do You Say That I Am?: Essays on Christology*. Louisville: Westminster John Knox, 1999.

Puosi, Eric E. "A Systematic Approach to the Christology of Peter's Address to the Crowd (Acts 2:14–36)." *New Blackfriars* 87:1009 (2006) 253–67.

Raven, Charles. *Apollinarianism: An Essay on the Christology of the Early Church*. New York: AMS, 1978.

Rees, Ian. "Exegesis: Prophecy and Scripture." *Evangel* 13 (1995) 36–38.

Richard, Earl J. "The Functional Christology of First Peter." In *Perspectives on First Peter*, edited by Charles H. Talbert, 121–39. Macon, GA: Mercer University Press, 1986.

Richards, W. L. "A Closer Look: Text und Textwert der Griechischen Handschriften des Neuen Testaments: Die Katholischen Briefe." *Andrews University Seminary Studies* 34 (1996) 37–46.

———. "The New Testament Greek Manuscripts of the Catholic Epistles." *Andrews University Seminary Studies* 14 (1976) 301–11.

———. "The Present Status of Text Critical Studies in the Catholic Epistles." *Andrews University Seminary Studies* 13 (1975) 261–72.

Rienecker, Fritz, and Cleon Rogers. *A Linguistic Key to the Greek New Testament*. Grand Rapids: Zondervan, 1980.

Riesner, Rainer. "Der zweite Petrus-Brief und die Eschatologie." In *Zukunftserwartung in biblischer Sicht: Beiträge zur Eschatologie*, edited by G. Maier, 124–43. Giessen, Germany: Brunnen, 1984.

Robbins, Vernon K. "Conceptual Blending and Early Christian Imagination." In *Explaining Christian Origins and Early Judaism*, edited by R. Alan Culpepper and Ellen von Wolde, 161–95. Leiden: Brill, 2007.

Roberts, J. W. "A Note on the Meaning of II Peter 3:10d." *Restoration Quarterly* 6 (1962) 32–33.

Robertson, Archibald Thomas. *Word Pictures in the New Testament*. Broadman & Holman, 1973. Logos 4, Scholars Library, Silver Edition. Oak Harbor, WA: Logos, 1997.

Robinson, John A. T. *Redating the New Testament*. Philadelphia: Westminster, 1976.

Rosenblatt, Marie-Eloise. "2 Peter." In *Searching the Scriptures: A Feminist Commentary*, edited by Elisabeth Schüssler Fiorenza, 2:399–405. New York: Crossroad, 1994.

Rowston, Douglas. "The Most Neglected Book in the New Testament." *New Testament Studies* 21 (1974) 554–63.

Russell, David Michael. "The 'New Heavens and New Earth': Hope for the Creation in Jewish Apocalyptic and the New Testament." PhD diss., Southwestern Baptist Theological Seminary, 1991.

Schaff, Philip, ed. *Early Church Fathers*. Vol. 12 in *Nicene and Post-Nicene Fathers*, series 1. Logos 4, Scholars Library, Silver Edition. Oak Harbor, WA: Logos, 1997.

Scharf, Kurt. "Zwei Versuche: Teilhabe des Unvergänglichen [Sermon on 1 Peter 1:3–9]; das Volk Israel und die Christen." In *Zeugnis und Dienst: Beiträge zu Theologie und Kirche in Geschichte und Gegenwart*, edited by Gottfried Sprondel, 223–30. Bremen, Germany: Schünemann Universitätsverlag, 1974.

Schrage, Wolfgang. "'Ein Tag ist beim Herrn wie tausend Jahre, und tausend Jahre sind wie ein Tag' (2 Petr 3,8)." In *Glaube und Eschatologie: Festschrift für Werner Georg Kümmel zum 80. Geburtstag*, edited by E. Grxbxb[umlaut over a]äßer and O. Merk, 267–75. Tübingen: Mohr Siebeck, 1985.

Schreiner, Thomas R. *1, 2 Peter, Jude*. New American Commentary 37. Nashville: Broadman & Holman, 2003.

Seifrid, Mark A. "The Near Word of Christ and the Distant Vision of N.T. Wright." *Journal of the Evangelical Theological Society* 54:2 (2011) 279–97.

Senior, Donald. "The Letters of Jude and 2 Peter." *The Bible Today* 25 (1987) 209–14.

Sherwood, John. "The Only Sure Word." *Master's Seminary Journal* 7:1 (1996) 53–74.

Sidebottom, E. M. *James, Jude and 2 Peter*. New Century Bible Commentary. London: Thomas Nelson, 1967.

Smith, David Paul. "Transforming Second Peter: A Historical Literary Rereading." PhD diss., Southern Baptist Theological Seminary, 1995.

Smith, Terence V. *Petrine Controversies in Early Christianity: Attitudes Towards Peter in Christian Writings of the First Two Centuries*. Wissenshaftlische Untersuchungen zum Neuen Testament 15. Tübingen: Mohr, 1985.

Snyder, John I. "A 2 Peter Bibliography." *Journal of the Evangelical Theological Society* 22 (1979) 265–67.

———. *The Promise of His Coming: The Eschatology of 2 Peter*. San Mateo, CA: Western, 1986.

Soards, Marion L. "1 Peter, 2 Peter and Jude as Evidence for a Petrine School." *Aufstieg und Niedergang der römischen Welt* 25:5 (1988) 3828–44.

Spence-Jones, H. D. M. *The Pulpit Commentary: 2 Peter*. Logos 4, Scholars Library, Silver Edition. Bellingham, WA: Logos, 2004.

Sproul, R. C. *1–2 Peter*. St. Andrew's Expositional Commentary. Wheaton, IL: Crossway, 2011.

Starr, James M. "Does 2 Peter 1:4 Speak of Deification?" In *Partakers of the Divine Nature*, edited by Michael J. Christensen and Jeffrey A. Wittung, 81–92. Grand Rapids: Baker, 2008.

Summerhill, James. "Assessing Open Theism's Christological Implications." PhD diss., Mid-America Baptist Theological Seminary, 2009.

Swanson, James. *Dictionary of Biblical Languages with Semantic Domains*. Logos 4, Scholars Library, Silver Edition. Bellingham, WA: Logos, 1997.

Talbert, Charles H., ed. *Perspectives on First Peter*. Macon, GA: Mercer University Press, 1986.

Thiede, Carsten Peter. "A Pagan Reader of 2 Peter: Cosmic Conflagration in 2 Peter 3 and the Octavius of Minucius Felix." *Journal for the Study of the New Testament* 26 (1986) 79–96.

———. "Style Never Goes Out of Fashion: 2 Peter Re-Evaluated." In *Rhetoric, Scripture and Theology: Essays from the 1994 Pretoria Conference*, edited by Stanley E. Porter and Thomas H. Olbricht, 329–47. Journal for the Study of the New Testament, Supplement Series 131. Sheffield: Sheffield Academic, 1996.

Titrud, Kermit. "The Function of καί in the Greek New Testament and an Application to 2 Peter." In *Linguistics and New Testament Interpretation: Essays on Discourse Analysis*, edited by David Alan Black, Katherine Barnwell, and Stephen Levinsohn, 240–70. Nashville: Broadman & Holman, 1992.

Utley, Robert James. *The Gospel according to Peter: Mark and I & II Peter*. Study Guide Commentary Series, New Testament 2. Marshall, TX: Bible Lessons International, 2000.

Vakarik, Antonij. "Excellent Glory: Sermon for the Transfiguration of the Lord." *Journal of the Moscow Patriarchate* 8 (1985) 39–40.

Van Rensburg, Fika J. "No Retaliation! An Ethical Analysis of the Exhortation in 1 Peter 3:9 Not to Repay Evil with Evil." In *Animosity, the Bible, and Us: Some European, North American, and South African Perspectives*, edited by John T. Fitzgerald, Fika J. van Rensburg, and Herrie F. van Rooy, 199–230. Atlanta: Society of Biblical Literature, 2009.

Vincent, Marvin Richardson. *Word Studies in the New Testament*. 1886. Logos 4, Scholars Library, Silver Edition. Bellingham, WA: Logos, 2002.

Vögtle, Anton. *Der Judasbrief; Der 2. Petrusbrief*. Evangelisch-katholischer Kommentar zum Neuen Testament 22. Solothurn, Switzerland: Benziger, 1994.

———. "Petrus und Paulus nach dem Zweiten Petrusbrief," "Die Schriftwerdung der apostolischen Paradosis nach 2 Petr 1,12–15," and "Keine Prophétie der Schrift ist Sache eigenwilliger Auslegung (2 Petr 1,20b)." In *Offenbarungsgeschehen und Wirkungsgeschichte: Neutestamentliche Beiträge*, edited by Anton Vögtle, 221–66, 297–304, 305–28. Freiburg: Herder, 1985.

Waard, Jan de, and Eugene A. Nida. *From One Language to Another: Functional Equivalence in Bible Translation*. Nashville: Nelson, 1987.

Walls, David, and Max Anders, eds. *1 and 2 Peter, 1, 2 and 3 John, Jude*. Holman New Testament Commentary. Nashville: Broadman & Holman, 1999.

Walvoord, John F., and Roy B. Zuck, eds. *The Bible Knowledge Commentary: An Exposition of the Scriptures*. Wheaton, IL: Victor, 1983.

Ward, Vanessa Oliver. "Addenda to Marion Soards: 1 & 2 Peter, Jude: Evidence for a Petrine School." *Aufstieg und Niedergang der römischen Welt* 25:5 (1988) 3844–49.

Watson, Duane F., and Terrance Callan. *First and Second Peter*. Paideia: Commentaries on the New Testament. Grand Rapids: Baker, 2012.

Webb, Robert L., and Duane F. Watson, eds. *Reading Second Peter with New Eyes: Methodological Reassessments of the Letter of Second Peter*. New York: T. & T. Clark, 2010.

Wenham, David. "Being 'Found' on the Last Day: New Light on 2 Peter 3.10 and 2 Corinthians 5.3." *New Testament Studies* 33 (1987) 477–79.

Wheatley-Irving, Linda. "The Miracles of the Messiah and Peter's Confession (Mark 7:31–9:1)." *Proceedings* (Eastern Great Lakes and Midwest Biblical Societies) 12 (199) 145–53.

White, L. Michael. "Adolf Harnack and the 'Expansion' of Early Christianity: A Reappraisal of Social History." *Second Century* 5 (1986) 97–127.

Wieland, George M. *The Significance of Salvation: A Study of Salvation Language in the Pastoral Epistles*. Milton Keynes: Paternoster, 2006.

Wikenhauser, Alfred. *New Testament Introduction*. Translated by Joseph Cunningham. New York: Herder, 1958.

Williams, Joel Stephen. "Inerrancy, Inspiration, and Dictation." *Restoration Quarterly* 37 (1995) 158–77.

Williams, Martin. *The Doctrine of Salvation in the First Letter of Peter*. Cambridge: Cambridge University Press, 2011.

Willmington, Harold L. "Peter's Two Epistles." *Fundamentalist Journal* 4:5 (1985) 59–318.

———. *Willmington's Bible Handbook*. Wheaton, IL: Tyndale, 1997.

Witherington, Ben, III. "A Petrine Source in 2 Peter." In *Society of Biblical Literature 1985 Seminar Papers*, edited by Kent Richards, 187–92. SBL Seminar Papers 24. Atlanta: Scholars, 1985.

———. *The Indelible Image: The Theological and Ethical Thought World of the New Testament*. Downers Grove, IL: InterVarsity, 2009.

Wolters, Albert M. "Partners of the Deity: A Covenantal Reading of 2 Peter 1:4." *Calvin Theological Journal* 25:1 (1990) 28–44.

———. "Postscript to 'Partners of the Deity.'" *Calvin Theological Journal* 26:2 (1991) 418–20.

———. "Worldview and Textual Criticism in 2 Peter 3:10." *Westminster Theological Journal* 49 (1987) 405–13.

Wright, N. T. *Jesus and the Victory of God*. London: SPCK, 1992.

Wuest, Kenneth S. *Wuest's Word Studies from the Greek New Testament.* Grand Rapids: Eerdmans, 1997.

Zahn, Theodor. *Introduction to the New Testament.* Translated by John Moor Trout. 3 vols. Grand Rapids: Kregel, 1953.

Zodhiates, Spiros. *The Complete Word Study Dictionary: New Testament.* Chattanooga, TN: AMG, 2000.

www.ingramcontent.com/pod-product-compliance
Lightning Source LLC
Chambersburg PA
CBHW070919160426
43193CB00011B/1519